THERE IS NO PLANET B:

Promise and Peril On Our Warming World

Trevor Greene

and

Mike Velemirovich

This book is dedicated to the memory of David James-Wilson.

David was a mentor to Trevor and Mike's wife Barb.
His huge heart, wisdom and spirit of compassion
lives on in his wife Sonia, his children, Symon and Matthew,
and the thousands of people he touched in his all too brief life.

To our beautiful wives Debbie and Barb, the
strongest and bravest people we know.
And to our children, Noah, Grace, Ella, Brett,
Victor and Taylor. And their children after them.

All proceeds from sales of this book
will be used to purchase carbon offsets for
the Great Bear Rainforest Project.

Trevor Greene and Mike Velemirovich

What can a decorated soldier and a "science nerd businessman" tell us about the state of the world's environment? Plenty. This is their passionate, opinionated, highly readable take on the whole earth catalogue of issues we all face as consumers, as parents, as citizens of the world. In 200 very readable pages Greene and Velemirovich whip us through the state of Canada's and the world's environment. Quoting academics, activists and Dr. Seuss they walk us through a wasteland of our own creation and find the little poppies on the battlefield that offer hope of averting an environmental Armageddon.

Ken MacQueen
Vancouver Bureau Chief, Maclean's

A powerful, passionate – and ultimately, hopeful – challenge to Canada's fossil-fueled status quo, Greene and Velemirovich cover the waterfront of new ideas with eyes on the prize of a sustainable future for all our children. This is a must-read for Canadians who think the environmental battle is already lost. And a welcome reminder to the rest of the world that so many Canadians, if not their government, long to embrace an alternative energy future.

Mitch Potter
Washington Bureau Chief Toronto Star

'There is no Planet B' is an important piece of civil disobedience written by two Canadians who want to challenge the orthodoxy of this country's addiction to producing and consuming non-renewables. Through a global survey of old, new and emerging technologies, Trevor and Mike provide the building blocks of a low carbon alternative version of the future. It should be read, absorbed and used.

Prof. James Tansey
Executive Director, ISIS, Sauder School of Business, UBC.

"As a Canadian I am proud of Captain Greene's spirit, fortitude and of the cause he has undertaken. As an auto executive I am disturbed at the haphazard and disparate manner in which vehicle emissions are being legislated (or not) in the different world markets, and equally concerned that environmentally unfriendly vehicles are still being mass-produced by some companies for those markets. There is a desperate need for the implementation of international standards so that automotive companies such as ours can accelerate the acceptance of affordable low emission vehicles worldwide. This presents a fantastic opportunity for Canada to re-take a leadership role and to shine on the world stage before it is too late."

John White
President and CEO, Volkswagen Group Australia.

"Anyone who knows anything of Captain Trevor Greene, the former Canadian Armed Forces soldier who wrote the bestselling memoir, March Forth, with his wife Debbie, will be utterly unsurprised to learn that he has for a moment been idle during his miraculous recovery. Anyone who

does not, should take heed that a man who was struck with an axe to the back of the head during his time in Afghanistan, has been profoundly worried not for his own fate but for that of his and our families and the Earth he calls 'Planet A.' In There is No Planet B, Greene and Volkswagen dealer, Mike Velemirovich, meticulously catalogue the injuries our fossil fuel-driven economies have been perpetrating upon the environment. They also write the history of how we arrived at this juncture, and the lies that governments and corporations would have us believe. But Greene and Velemirovich provide reasons for hope, too, all in a style that is animated and entertaining throughout. Human beings are smart enough to have gotten ourselves into this mess, so we should be smart enough to get out ourselves of it. Their urgent and impassioned defense of Planet A is first proof that we can. Read this book and bring on more."

Noah Richler
Bestselling author and journalist. Richler's latest book, *What We Talk About When We Talk About War*, was published in April 2012.

When an auto executive and an Afghan war veteran collaborate to write about climate change and the state of our society, you can expect the sparks to fly. They do! Insightful, fascinating, and informative, I highly recommend this book to climate change deniers, skeptics, and believers alike.

Dr. Brian Nattrass
Coauthor of The Natural Step for Business and Dancing With the Tiger; Batten Fellow, Darden Graduate School of Business; Managing Partner, Sustainability Partners

Trevor Greene and Mike Velemirovich

TABLE OF CONTENTS

FOREWORD

By Dr. David Suzuki

Canadians are proud of the country's record as peacekeepers and defenders of human rights. Trevor Greene, as a member of Canada's armed forces, went to Afghanistan, believing in those high values and the hope of spreading them to the beleaguered people of that poor nation. He paid a heavy price while speaking to village elders when a terrorist planted an axe in his brain. Trevor not only survived this appalling wound, but after long months of rehabilitation, astounded the medical profession with his recovery. But the Canada to which he returned had changed from the one whose values he set out to spread.

The Great Depression following the stock market crash of 1929, was a time of widespread suffering around the planet, a painful warning of the hazards in a world increasingly enmeshed in global economics. The great economist, John Maynard Keynes, advised long ago: "Ideas, knowledge, art, hospitality, travel—these are the things which should of their nature be international. But let goods be homespun whenever it is reasonably and conveniently possible; and, above all, let finance be national."

What brought North America, especially the United States, out of the Depression was the Japanese attack on Pearl Harbour in 1941. War can be a stimulus for weapons production, demand for manpower and innovation, raw material for a hungry economy.

For me and my family, BC-born and raised, December 7th signified a different fate. Branding us as potential enemies, solely on the basis of racial identity, the state invoked the War Measures Act depriving Japanese-Canadians of all rights of citizenship — freedom of speech and movement, frozen accounts, confiscated assets. JCs were ordered from homes, housed in hastily constructed makeshift facilities like the cattle barns in Hastings Park.

The most difficult challenge for a democracy is that while it's easy to guarantee the sanctity of free speech, movement and equal rights when times are good, the only time those guarantees matter are when times are tough. Canada (and the United States) failed to uphold those rights for citizens of Japanese descent, thereby creating different categories of citizenship. The government claimed it was defending the country against a perceived enemy, a fine aspiration, but surely those ends do not justify the suspension of the very foundation on which that democracy is based. Ends cannot justify ends, as Prime Minister Mulroney's 1988 apology to Japanese-Canadians indicated.

In times of stress, what is most precious to society is diversity of ideas, not enforced uniformity.

Do we learn from history? Despite Keynes' prescient advice, economic globalization has proceeded at full speed. After World War II, the American economy boomed and it seemed the American dream was achievable by all. The promise of limitless growth and opportunity beckoned irresistibly. The problem is this rationale is based on a single notion of development and progress, a belief that with growth, the benefits will trickle down to raise all.

The past five decades have been a period of unprecedented growth as corporations have become richer and more powerful than most governments and through funding of politicians and lobbying, these corporations have eventually come to dictate government priorities and actions. Wealth has flowed up, rather than trickling down, both

Trevor Greene and Mike Velemirovich

within nations and between them as corporations sought benefits from no regulations, low taxes, minimal environmental and workplace protection.

The past 50 years have also been a period of explosive growth in the environmental movement. It was Rachel Carson's seminal book, *Silent Spring*, published in 1962 that created a modern environmental movement. All about the unexpected effects of pesticides like DDT, her book ended the uncritical optimism about technological "progress." Remember, when Paul Mueller discovered that DDT kills insects, it was embraced as a demonstration of our ability to control through science some of the great problems that we had lived with since the beginning of time. Mueller won a Nobel prize in 1948. Carson pointed out that the lab is not a miniature replica of the world around us, it is a gross simplification that cannot anticipate the consequences like bio-magnification of applying powerful technologies.

When Carson's book was published, there wasn't a department of the environment in any government in the world. She put the environment on the agenda and in only ten years, millions of people worldwide had been swept up in the movement, the UN called the first world conference on the environment in Stockholm and formed the United Nations Environment Program.

Oil spills from supertankers, dioxin release in Seveso, Italy, the chemical leak in Bhopal, India, the fire in Basel, Switzerland, that released chemicals and sterilized the Rhine River, mercury pollution in Minamata, Japan and Grassy Narrows Ontario, fires at Three Mile Island and Chernobyl, all increased public concern about the environment.

By 1988, the environment had achieved top status as an issue of concern. Indeed, a U.S. candidate for political office promised to "be an environmental president" if elected. George H.W. Bush didn't have a green bone in his body but had to say that because the American people cared. That same year, Brian Mulroney was re-elected Prime Minister of Canada and to demonstrate his environmental concern, appointed his brightest star, Lucien Bouchard, as Environment Minister. When I interviewed Bouchard a few months later, I asked him what he felt was the most important environmental issue facing Canadians. He immediately answered "global warming." When I then asked how serious it was, he replied "it threatens the survival of our species. We have to act now." That was impressive.

In 1988, the Intergovernmental Panel on Climate Change [IPCC] was established to review the literature and assess the state of the planet's climate. In 1992, the largest gathering of heads of state in human history attended the Earth Summit in Rio de Janeiro Brazil. It had a plan, Agenda 21, to move humanity onto a different path to sustainability. In 1997, leaders met in Kyoto, Japan, to deal with what the IPCC had declared was the real problem of humanity's contribution to climate change.

Despite laws to protect the planet's air, water, soil and endangered species, and millions of hectares of land protected in parks and reserves, we continued on our destructive path, but now giant corporations and billionaires began to spend tens of millions on a highly successful campaign of deception and confusion that created the illusion that scientists had agendas other than telling the truth and that issues like the human contribution to climate change were still not settled.

In 2001, Prime Minister Jean Chretien ratified the Kyoto Protocol

Trevor Greene and Mike Velemirovich

and committed Canada to meeting the 2010 target of a 5 – 6% reduction from 1990 levels of greenhouse gas emissions. Upon elevation to Prime Minister in 2006, Stephen Harper overturned the programs to reduce emissions and announced that Canada would not attempt to meet the Kyoto commitments because to do so would be bad for the economy. In 2011, with a majority government, despite his declared commitment to law and order, Harper withdrew from the international Kyoto treaty.

Of all industrialized countries, Canada is probably the most vulnerable to the effects of climate change. It is a northern nation and we know that warming is much greater towards the poles. Inuit people have been informing us of the palpable changes for decades. With the longest marine coastline of any country, Canada will be most affected by sea level rise. And climate-sensitive areas of agriculture, forestry, fisheries, tourism and winter sports all call for action on mitigating climate change.

The Harper government's response to the challenge of climate change is to ignore it as an issue of importance, concentrating instead on the economic importance of sectors like energy and forestry that are contributing to the problem. Perhaps most egregious is the shutting down of sources of information relevant to the issue of climate and other environmental challenges. Cancelling the mandatory long-form census means we have no solid data on the country on which to plan strategies into the future. Cancelling activities designed to provide information relevant to climate, such as the Experimental Lakes Area and polar research while muzzling scientists and vetting their reports, has become the modus operandi of the government (Chris Turner's 2013 *Harper's War on Science*).

The strongest source of information about climate change is environmental non-governmental organizations (ENGOs) who take the arcane reports of scientists and translate them into everyday vernacular along with strong suggestions for solving the problem. Harper's ministers have labelled ENGOs as "radical extremists", accused them of "laundering foreign money" and linked them to terrorist organizations.

The consequence of this is that the Canadian government has not acknowledged the reality of human-induced climate change and thus has no serious plan to reduce greenhouse gas emissions. Canada and Canadians like Maurice Strong have been acknowledged leaders in the movement but that reputation has been squandered since the Harper years. At the Rio+20 conference in 2012, a young female delegate from Canada recounted in tears that she had just come from an elevator where she had joined a group from Africa. One of the Africans read her nametag and surmised "Oh you are from Canada?" to which she nodded then was stunned when he shot back, "why do you bother coming? Canada is not serious about these issues." Year after year, at international conferences on climate change, Canada has been designated "fossil" of the day, week and year.

This then is the history to the present that has motivated Trevor Greene and his friend, Mike Velemirovich, to write their book. Planet B delves into all aspects of the global warming issue all over the world through the eyes of Trevor, a soldier, and Mike, an auto industry veteran. I hope they find a large Canadian audience.

When all the trees have been cut down, when all the animals have been hunted, when all the waters are polluted, when all the air is unsafe to breathe, only then will you discover you cannot eat money

~ Cree Prophecy

PROLOGUE

Mike: In the spring of 2003 on the final day of a Florida vacation, my then seven-year old son convinced me to go for one last swim. I figured he would be okay without sunscreen, because we would only be outside for an hour and besides, I had played outside without sunscreen all day when I was his age. I was wrong and he suffered sunburn. As my little boy moaned his way to sleep, I realized our world had changed and my family's car business that gave us a comfortable life was partly responsible, since we sell the cars that burn the fuel that harms the environment. My guilt went beyond the sunscreen and deepened as I recalled taking part in lobbying efforts to relax emissions standards and working on corporate advertising teams that wielded multi-million dollar budgets to drive new car demand. Like Charles Dickens' Ebenezer Scrooge, the guilt of business past weighed heavily on me and pushed me to find a better way.

Trevor: We are not professional environmentalists, just ordinary Canadians who care about our children and the planet they've lent us. It was that kind of thinking that led me to Afghanistan because I believed in Canada and our commitment to environmental and social justice issues and wanted to share cherished Canadian values with others. I was severely injured in an axe attack on my 50th day in-theatre. I barely survived and was returned to Canada in a coma. When I came out of my coma and regained my wits, I was shocked, then outraged, by the transformation in my homeland. My government seems to have become obsessed with exploitation of the tar sands and everything else be damned. Oil sands special interests seem to be driving government policy instead of the other way round and Canada is increasingly being described as a burgeoning petro-state.

Russia is firmly in the ranks of the petro-states and is going hard after Arctic oil. According to some estimates, the Arctic is home to a quarter of the world's untapped energy reserves. The five nations on the Arctic Ocean, Russia, Norway, Canada, the United States (through Alaska) and Denmark (through Greenland) have rightful claims to 200 miles of territorial waters in the Arctic. Since the Soviet era, Russia has held claim to a chunk of the Arctic about the size of Western Europe. In a bid to claim these reserves for Russia once and for all, one of their submarines planted a Russian flag on the seafloor in August 2007.

On September 18th 2013, 30 Greenpeace activists attempted to board an oilrig operated by Russian energy giant Gazprom in the eastern Arctic. The Russian Coast Guard boarded the Greenpeace ship in international waters and towed her to port. Initially, all 30 were charged with piracy, which carries a sentence of 15 years. In October, the charge was lessened to hooliganism, with a sentence of seven years. The activists, who became known as the Arctic 30, were detained for two months in Murmansk. The charge of piracy implied that the unarmed Greenpeacers' intent was to seize control of the rig or steal property. I [Trevor] suspect incidents like the Arctic 30 will become more and more common in the coming years and will lead to bloodshed and possibly armed conflict which could spiral out of control as the cause of the conflict gets forgotten. When I was working as a journalist, I of course was aware of the nature of conflict and war, but unless I was covering it, the causes of the various conflicts were always hazy. The cause of my war is indelibly emblazoned on the global collective memory; everyone remembers where they were when those airplanes sliced into the World Trade Centre towers. But I think future conflicts will have a common theme: climate change. Later in the book, we will discuss how the causes of the bloody Arab Spring uprisings of 2011 were only superficially political. One month before the uprisings in the Middle East and North Africa, food prices in Egypt and Tunisia soared to record highs. Award-winning journalist and top-flight geopolitical analyst, Gwynne Dyer, wrote a prescient book, *Climate Wars*, in 2011. Dyer predicted that over the next 15 to 20 years, climate change will drive the world powers to ever more desperate measures to secure food and water resources. Specifically, Dyer points to tension over jurisdiction of shrinking river systems between India and Pakistan, Iraq and Turkey, and Chinese control over the headwaters of several important rivers that are critical to Southeast Asian food production.

We often hear people say the fight against climate change has been lost and take that as license to stop caring for our precious planet. We are convinced there is a better way forward and that is why we wrote this book. We wanted to admit defeats but inspire hope and tout the many victories. We wanted to show that for every business that harms our world, there are others working to defend and improve it. We wanted to discuss the folly of hinging the economy on a fossil-fueled future. We wanted to show that Planet A is still worth fighting for.

WHY WE ARE EXTREMISTS

We are extremists. We are extremists like hundreds of concerned scientists, hockey legend Scott Niedermayer, star economist Jeff Rubin and tens of thousands of law-abiding, tax-paying citizens across the country. In February 2012, Minister of Public Safety Vic Toews released Canada's first counter-terrorism strategy. The report labeled environmentalism as "an example of domestic issue-based extremism, like white supremacy activities and domestic bombing." The only thing we extremists have in common is membership in an environmental group. To quote from the paper:

> *Such extremism tends to be based on grievances - real or perceived - revolving around the promotion of various causes such as animal rights, white supremacy, environmentalism and anti-capitalism.* [Toronto Star]

It feels disturbing and surreal that our government lumps us in with white supremacists and domestic terrorists because we care for the environment. Toews and his ilk would do well to revisit lessons learned at story time.

A CAUTIONARY TALE FROM DR. SEUSS

The Dr. Seuss classics hold many life lessons. *Oh the Places You'll Go* is a primer on dealing with life's confusion, choices and how to take responsibility for your own life. Another is *The Lorax*, a cautionary tale about corporate greed destroying the environment. Written in 1971, long before the environment became a global issue, the story is about a young boy in a badly polluted world who meets an industrialist, called the Once-ler, and asks how the world got so foul. He tells the boy about how the world was once beautiful, with happy animals that lived among the 'Truffula' trees. But the Once-ler invented a product called Thneeds, made from Truffula trees. Thneeds became very popular so the Once-ler expanded his factory and cut down more trees. An orange dwarf called the Lorax appears one day and declares his mission:

I am the Lorax. I speak for the trees. I speak for the trees for the trees have no tongues.

The Lorax warns the Once-ler that animals need the trees to survive. The Once-ler ignores this sage advice and expands his business a hundredfold:

I meant no harm. I most truly did not.

But I had to grow bigger. So bigger I got.

I biggered my factory. I biggered the roads.

I biggered my wagons. I biggered the loads.

Inevitably, the land becomes polluted and gray. Soon, the Truffula trees are all cut down:

From outside in the fields came a sickening smack

Of an axe on a tree. Then we heard the tree fall.

The very last Truffula Tree of them all

With his only raw material gone, the Once-ler goes out of business and has to close his factory. The Lorax disappears and the Once-ler is left to look over with remorse the formerly idyllic landscape he ruined. He tosses the boy the last Truffula seed:

Plant a new Truffula. Treat it with care.

Give it clean water. And feed it clean air.

Grow a forest. Protect it from axes that hack.

I [Trevor] was born in Sydney, Nova Scotia in the heart of Cape Breton's coal belt. The steel mill in Sydney created the Sydney tar ponds, Canada's most infamous toxic waste site. Sydney was the perfect location for a steelworks. Hundreds of thousands of miles of coal seams snaked underground, nearby Newfoundland had a wealth of iron ore and limestone for smelting, Sydney had a fine, deep harbour and plenty of water to cool the superheated metal. The mill produced half of Canada's steel by 1912. Generations of sons followed their fathers into the best-paying job in town. Sydney residents paid a hard price for their bounty: per capita cancer rates are 16 per cent higher in Sydney than anywhere else in Canada. Steel is made by smelting iron ore with coke and limestone in coke ovens. The Sydney coke ovens were in continuous use from 1901 to 1988. When the ovens were examined, over 150 kilometres of pipes carrying toxic, explosive chemicals and coke waste were found. In 2004, Sydney found their metaphorical Truffula seed when the federal and provincial governments began a 10-year cleanup project. Open Hearth Park opened right on time on August 29th

2013 with three kilometres of paved walking trails, a playground and an artificial athletic field.

In the US, the publication of The Lorax preceded the Clean Water Act of 1972 and the Endangered Species Act of 1973, which coincided with the mass anti-Vietnam War demonstrations that forced the US to pull out of Vietnam and proved to a whole generation that focusing energy and idealism in large numbers could effect change. The 1970s saw an explosion in the number of environmental organizations. President Jimmy Carter installed solar panels on the White House roof predicting America could harness the power of the sun to break its dependence on foreign oil, but with Texas oilman George Bush Sr. as vice president, President Ronald Reagan had the solar panels removed. By the mid 2000s oil was becoming harder to find and so expensive that the industry began extracting thick, barely viscous petroleum called bitumen from oil sands. The Athabasca oil sands contain petroleum reserves second only in the world to Saudi Arabia. Just as Sydney steel did for Cape Breton, the oil sands offer enormous prosperity for Alberta's sons and daughters. But the process involves the strip-mining of thousands of hectares of boreal forest and the creation of tailings ponds larger than some cities. The spike in oil costs that ignited oil sands production also brought about renewed interest in the environment. Huge numbers of people in nations around the world are once again focusing their idealism on the environment. The Once-lers of the oil industry biggered their voices in the 1980s, but modern environmentalists have learned to lobby just as effectively and since policy makers follow large numbers of energized people, the Lorax's sage advice rings true:

Unless someone like you cares a whole awful lot
nothing is going to get better. It's not.

Trevor Greene and Mike Velemirovich

OUR MISSIONS

FIGHTING FOR MY CHILDREN'S FUTURE

I am a soldier. I watched with the rest of the world in stunned, impotent silence as two airplanes destroyed the World Trade Centre towers. I knew that the people who had turned innocuous passenger planes into weapons and had meticulously planned such an atrocity had to be cruel fanatics. I knew retribution would be swift and I knew I had to be in on the fight. My mission in Afghanistan as a Civil-Military Cooperation officer was to find out what local villagers needed for the necessities of life and provide for those needs. I soon learned that empowerment and education, not handouts, are the keys to restoring peace and prosperity to Afghanistan. Education is the key to freeing Afghans from dependence on murderous thugs like the Taliban and I was constantly asking stony-faced elders if they would let girls attend if I built them a school. Journalists identified the boy who swung an axe into my skull as Abdul Karim, an uneducated peasant who had undoubtedly not read the Koran. Abdul would have been easy fodder for the Taliban, who could have easily convinced him that the only way to reach Paradise was to kill an infidel. Ironically, Abdul was just the kind of young man I was there to help by building schools. A teacher could have taught Abdul to read the Koran, a holy book that teaches that the way to Paradise is to live with compassion and love in your heart. The rich nations pumping carbon into the atmosphere causing climate change would do well to study and apply these lessons, because it is poor, strife-torn countries like Afghanistan and peasants like Abdul that will suffer and die for our indifference and greed. I began my military career in the regular force Navy. The highlight of my short naval career was crossing the Pacific Ocean on the Navy's tall ship, HMCS Oriole. I could tell where we were by fixing our position but immediately knew we were approaching port when we started sailing through the ubiquitous garbage and oil scum. It was a starkly disturbing contrast to the clean, fresh wildness of the open ocean. This book consumed me for over a year for one main reason: in her book *Raising Elijah*, ecologist Sandra Steingraber paints a picture from Cold War America in which a grade-school teacher asks the kids in her class if they are afraid of nuclear destruction. Every hand in the class flies up except for a sister and brother. Curious, the teacher asks them why they aren't worried. The kids reply that their parents are anti-war campaigners and are doing something about the threat. If my children's teacher asks their class if they fear environmental devastation, I want them to keep their hands down.

THE EPIPHANY OF A SCIENCE NERD BUSINESSMAN

Before entering the car business, my high school recreational reading included Isaac Asimov and Carl Sagan and I went on to study physics and astronomy at the University of Toronto where I chose elective courses like oceanography: I was a science nerd. My search to find a better way for the auto industry led me to research resource depletion and climate change. In my generation, the global population doubled while the number of cars in the world increased fivefold and it became clear that human activity was harming the environment. As a VW dealer who sold diesel cars, it occurred to me that biodiesel was an obvious first step. After all, in the late 1800s Dr. Rudolf Diesel invented his car engine to run on peanut oil. I ordered a 200-litre drum of industrial quality, pure biodiesel and the technicians in our shop cringed as I poured soybean biodiesel into the tank of a brand new 2003 Beetle. They were convinced the motor would give out or at the very least the fuel pump would seize. Their skepticism was understandable, because over the years they had seen more than a few well-intentioned, if not well-informed environmentalists damage their diesel engines by refueling with used cooking oil; fuel filters are not generally designed to handle French fry crumbs. These technicians made careers out of fixing internal combustion engines that ran on fossil fuel and that was the way the auto industry had operated for a hundred years, so the notion that a diesel engine would run on pure vegetable oil seemed absurd. As the technicians knelt down to smell the Beetle's exhaust, I think they expected soybeans to shoot out of the tailpipe. Their skepticism began to wane once I reminded them that fossil fuel and biofuel are both made from carbon-based plant material. Fossil fuel undergoes pressure and heat deep underground for millions of years while biofuel is harvested from above ground. People lined up to drive the "Bio Bug", so in no time at all I had burned through all 200 litres of biodiesel driving 3,000 kilometres at the same consumption rate as fossil fuel. And without a single mechanical problem.

Trevor Greene and Mike Velemirovich

DYING CANARIES

Most of the metaphorical canaries in the coalmine that warn of extreme environmental degradation are either dead or in palliative care. There is overwhelming evidence that global warming is toasting the globe. Scientists from the eight Arctic nations came to that chilling conclusion in a 2004 report that predicted the polar bear would not survive an ice-free arctic. The top of the food chain at the top of the world, polar bears are the first animals to feel the heat. Their food source is seals, which live in the arctic sea ice. Global warming is melting the sea ice and the bears are unable to catch their prey in open water. Adult polar bears can swim long distances, but with the ice melting, they have fewer places to rest and eat. Cubs have to travel everywhere with their mothers in the first two years, but many cubs, with less fat reserves, die because they are weaker and get colder.

A key sub-Arctic region that was the last bastion from global warming has fallen and is warming up, according to an October 2013 report by a Queen's University biologist. A bottleneck of ice on the western shore of Hudson Bay and James Bay kept the Hudson Bay Lowlands, a vast wetlands of lakes, rivers, peat bogs and polar bears, cool until the mid-90s. In the past 15 years, the Lowlands have warmed an average of 15 degrees.

The summer Arctic ice pack has receded to unprecedented levels yet again, raising the spectre of transit of an ice-free Northwest Passage by oil tanker. The Arctic heats up faster than the rest of the earth. As the ice cap melts, the energy of the sun is absorbed by the dark seawater, rather than reflected by the ice. This speeds climate change and warms the oceans. Melting permafrost releases methane, a greenhouse gas far more potent than carbon dioxide. Experts say the Arctic sea ice is in danger of disappearing entirely by 2016.

DEAD BEES AND BLEACHED CORAL

The ubiquitous honeybee is pointing the way as well. The phrase "colony collapse syndrome" was coined in 2006 when scientists found that honeybees were disappearing at an alarming rate. It's been a mystery that scientists have struggled to unravel, but the top three suspects are malnutrition, pesticides and genetically modified crops. Bee pollination is worth an estimated $15 billion in the US.

In March 2012, Mother Jones journalist Tom Philpott reported on three separate studies that fingered nicotine-derived pesticides made by the German chemical giant Bayer and used widely on the immense US corn crop. Philpott reported on another paper published in July 2013 that found that fungicides — widely thought to be "typically fairly safe for honey bees" — were weakening bees and making them more susceptible to a fungal pathogen closely linked to colony collapse disorder.

Bleached, lifeless coral reefs are another stark indicator. Coral bleaching is caused by warming oceans, increased ultraviolet radiation and so-called cyanide fishing where fishers squirt poison on the coral to stun reef fish prized by aquariums and Asian restaurants. In the Florida Keys, the U.S. Virgin Islands and Puerto Rico, less than 15 per cent of the coral is alive. In their attempt to get the message out and ignite meaningful debate, most environmental groups seem unable to avoid shrill "the-sky-is-falling" rhetoric, which dilutes their message and renders them largely ineffective. Meanwhile governments are allowing big business to flout environmental regulations meant to restrict the burning of fossil fuels. These businesses pay huge fees to lobby groups to be more effective than the environmentalists at influencing regulations.

THE ONSLAUGHT OF JUAN

Just after midnight on September 29th, 2003 a Category-2 hurricane with sustained winds of over 180 kilometres per hour slammed into my [Mike] hometown, Halifax, Nova Scotia. As my young children slept, oblivious to the storm, I heard what sounded like a dozen freight trains roaring through our yard. The entire house shook and the windows rattled as debris from falling trees struck the house. And then suddenly it was eerily quiet. I thought the storm had past, but the eye of the giant hurricane was 35 kilometres wide and passing right over the city. Moments later the raging wind and deafening noise began again as Hurricane Juan continued his terrible path. The storm was so destructive that the name Juan was retired from use in naming hurricanes. The storm surge wrecked wharves and damaged buildings all along Halifax's historic waterfront. Insurers defined a tide line along the Halifax waterfront below which real estate developers had to construct new buildings to be watertight in order to mitigate damage from rising tides and storm surges. The line extends beyond the harbour-hugging Lower Water Street to include the famous tourist attraction Historic Properties and one of Halifax's most beloved pubs, the Lower Deck, where Trevor and I have enjoyed many a pint and a song.

A COUPLE OF 'THOUSAND-YEAR STORMS' IN TWO YEARS

Hurricanes of unusually large size and extreme winds are often described with apocalyptic phrases like hundred- or thousand-year storms. In the few years that followed Juan, the Atlantic saw a series of epic storms erupt that further raised the question of just how much influence people have had on climate and the ferocity of weather. In August 2005, Katrina was just such a storm. A category-5 hurricane packing sustained winds of 280 kilometres per hour, Katrina was the fourth most intense Atlantic storm in recorded history. Katrina killed over 1,800 people and caused over $100 billion in damage. The intensity of Katrina was eclipsed later in that same season: hurricanes Rita, the 4th most severe hurricane, and Wilma, the most intense tropical cyclone ever recorded, outdid even Katrina's ferocity. Nature was demonstrating in dramatic fashion just how much influence human behaviour has on our natural world.

THE CIVILIZED ROAD UNTAKEN

Noted environmentalist Bill McKibben, founder of the climate change campaign 350.org, suggested that hurricanes be named after "the fossil fuel companies who have played the biggest role in making sure we don't slow global warming down." Companies like Enron and British Petroleum have for many years been shoveling millions of dollars to climate change deniers and anti-environment lobbyists in the US Congress. McKibben said, "at the very least it's fun to imagine the newscasters announcing, 'Exxon is coming ashore across New Jersey, leaving havoc in her wake', or 'Chevron forces evacuation of 375,000.'" McKibben commented in the March 2012 New York Review of Books that, "we could, as a civilization, have taken that dwindling supply and rising price [of fossil fuels] as a signal to convert to sun, wind, and other noncarbon forms of energy. It would have made eminent sense, most of all because it would have aided in the fight against global warming, the most difficult challenge the planet faces."

Mankind, alas, didn't do the civilized thing.

McKibben explained just how uncivilized we have become; "getting at [the remaining conventional energy sources] requires ripping apart the earth: for instance, by heating up the ground so that the oil in the tar sands formations of Canada can flow to the surface. Or by tearing holes in the Earth's crust a mile beneath the surface of the sea, as BP was doing in the Gulf of Mexico when the Deepwater Horizon well exploded. Or by literally removing mountaintops to get at coal, as has become commonplace across the southern Appalachians."

SUPERSTORM POLITICS

As the heat waves of 2006 killed tens of thousands of people worldwide, the message was clear: climate change cannot be ignored. People from all walks of life demanded action from corporations and from political leaders. As the green economy began to emerge, corporate legends like Jack Welch of General Electric told the 2006 graduating class of the Massachusetts Institute of Technology that, "green is the new black." Clean technology was worth $1 trillion in 2010. Barak Obama won the 2008 presidential election with a platform that included climate change as a major component and during his first term moved public policy toward a more sustainable society. With the persistent after-effects of the economic recession of 2008 still reverberating through American society, the 2012 presidential election was being touted as the most important election in history and yet climate change wasn't mentioned once during the debates between Obama and Mitt Romney. However, just a week before election night, the largest Atlantic storm in history with a diameter of 1,800 kilometres rolled up the eastern seaboard and took an abrupt turn left slamming into the media capital of the world, New York City. Hurricane Sandy killed 180 people, caused over $50 billion in damage and left millions of people without power for more than a week. As the US cleaned up and grieved, outspoken movie director, Oliver Stone said of hurricane Sandy, "this is punishment. Mother Nature cannot be ignored." New York City's pro-business conservative mayor, Michael Bloomberg, then endorsed President Obama specifically citing the need for leadership from the White House on environmental issues. "Make no mistake: This is a defining challenge for our future, and if anyone is up to the task of defending and adapting the city they love, it's New Yorkers," Bloomberg said. A canary named Sandy helped President Obama decisively win a second term in the White House and reminded North America that neither climate change nor nature can be ignored.

Trevor Greene and Mike Velemirovich

RISKY OIL

Salt has always played an integral role in civilization. It allowed for the preservation of food, which enabled people to travel over long distances and cross oceans. Salt was such a rare commodity in ancient times the Romans levied a tax on it to fund military campaigns. Natural gas was another commodity discovered in ancient times seeping to the Earth's surface through rock fissures. Flames erupting from the rocks were called eternal fires and have been the subject of mythology and superstition for thousands of years. About 500 BC, the Chinese developed a practical application for this naturally occurring gas: boiling heavily salted water called brine to produce salt. The natural gas was transported to salt production facilities through twine-reinforced bamboo: the first recorded fuel pipelines over 2,500 years ago. Today there are hundreds of thousands of kilometres of pipelines that have been moving fossil fuel throughout North America for over a century. Pipelines are the preferred method of transporting petroleum products because they are safer and have a smaller greenhouse gas footprint than either trucks or trains.

The Enbridge Northern Gateway Pipelines Project is a proposal by Calgary-based pipeline company Enbridge Inc. to build a 1,170-kilometre pipeline through the Rocky Mountains from Bruderheim, Alberta to Kitimat, British Columbia. The pipeline is intended to carry 525,000 barrels a day of liquefied tar sands called 'bitumen' to Kitimat on the central BC coast, where it will be loaded into huge oil freighters to be shipped to Asia. Since it was announced in 2006, the project has been postponed several times and aroused the intense ire of environmental groups, citizens of both provinces and First Nations.

WHAT ELSE ARE THEY LYING ABOUT?

Enbridge released a bird's eye-view video in August 2012 of the proposed route of the Northern Gateway. It's fairly routine until Kitimat, the western terminus, where the bitumen is to be loaded into tankers. The video shows a wide, ship-friendly Douglas Channel with nary an island in sight. The actual, non-Disneyesque channel is a narrow, island-studded mariner's nightmare. In its Marine Weather Hazards Manual, Environment Canada notes that Hecate Strait, where Douglas Channel meets the ocean, is considered the fourth most dangerous waterway in the world. Category-3 hurricane-force winds are common in the area. In the winter, furious gusts generate waves six to eight metres high. My [Trevor's] father-in-law is a commercial fisherman who has fished the waters around the Hecate Strait since the 1960s. Joe says he had to be careful piloting his 40-foot gillnetter because the waters are "kinda narrow and hairy." The proposed route would have giant oil tankers make an 'S' turn between two tiny islands into an aptly named Squally Channel after threading their way through the narrows of Douglas Channel. As he traces the route on his weathered nautical chart with his finger, Joe winces every time he comes to a particularly tight or shallow spot. By the time he gets to the open ocean, you'd think he was being poked with a fork. He painfully points to the 'S' turn as the spot where the tankers are in the most danger, "**if** they make it that far," he says through pursed lips. Every year, 225 immense Very Large Crude Carriers (VLCCs) - at 1,100 feet the length of the Eiffel Tower - will have to pick their way through that channel to get to the Pacific in the most extreme, sphincter-tightening weather on the west coast. VLCCs carry hundreds of thousands of barrels of toxic bitumen. A fully loaded VLCC travels at 18 mph and takes almost two kilometres to make a turn and three to make a full stop. There are spots where the route is less than two kilometres wide. As if that wasn't enough, VLCCs need at least 33 metres of water, but will have to scrape over one spot only 35 metres deep. The Exxon Valdez ran aground 23 years ago. That tanker, navigating less-dangerous waters, was only a few hundred feet shorter than a VLCC. In 1972, the Trudeau government banned crude oil tankers from northern British Columbia's coastal waters to protect the area from an oil spill. That's why there are no specific safeguards or emergency protocols in place in the event of a spill.

MORE RISK, WAY MORE RISK

Robyn Allan was the President and CEO of the Insurance Corporation of British Columbia and Senior Economist for B.C. Central Credit Union. In a presentation on the economics of oil tankers and pipelines in March 2013, she said Northern Gateway is intended to transport 525,000 barrels a day of crude oil. Allan said Northern Gateway would simply add pumping power to eventually increase crude oil capacity by 60%. "And the supertankers needed to transport it? Well its not 220 a year, but closer to 340 a year—almost two supertanker transits a day in BC's northern coastal waters," Allan says. "More crude. More tankers. More risk. Way more risk." On her website, Allan listed the many costs—not just economic—of the pipeline:

1. Decades of higher oil prices for Canadian consumers and businesses across the country;

2. Lost opportunity to add value, create meaningful jobs and control

environmental standards here at home;

3. Hollowing out of the oil sector as raw bitumen exports take precedence over upgrading and refining;

4. Twice the number of pipelines and almost double the tanker traffic to move diluted bitumen as compared to upgraded bitumen;

5. Supernatural British Columbia becomes a Supertanker terminal for Alberta.

She has harsh words for what she calls the oil interests who "deliberately mislead, misrepresent, and obfuscate in order to exaggerate benefits, deny the costs and underplay the environmental risk. We are told half-truths, we are made false promises, and since our needs and concerns are inconvenient we are viewed with contempt." The National Energy Board [NEB] is an independent federal agency that regulates pipelines, energy development and trade. In early 2010, the NEB set up a three-member Joint Review Panel to conduct a review of the proposed Enbridge Northern Gateway Project.

LOST OPPORTUNITIES, DECEPTION AND THE JOBS MYTH
Allan submitted a report to the NEB in January 2012 about the economic consequences of Northern Gateway on Canadians. We have excerpted the executive summary of her report *An Economic Assessment of Northern Gateway.*

"Enbridge has misrepresented Northern Gateway to the public and the project is neither needed nor is it in the public interest. The project represents serious economic risk to the Canadian economy. Unless Northern Gateway increases oil prices for Canadians there is no industry benefit and hence no economic benefit. Northern Gateway means lost opportunity to create a long-term energy security strategy

Trevor Greene and Mike Velemirovich

for Canadians. It also represents a lost opportunity to ensure reasoned and sustainable development of crude oil resources that captures real value-added in an environmentally responsible manner for the benefit of all Canadians. From a public policy standpoint, Canada is being outplayed."

The pipeline cuts through an area of the central BC coast that environmentalists call the 'Great Bear Rainforest,' the largest intact temperate rainforest remaining in the world. The region supports thousands of jobs in tourism. Marine tourism alone generates $104.3 million in revenues and provides 2,200 long-term jobs. These jobs will be threatened by the tanker traffic required to move diluted bitumen to the Pacific, not to mention what will happen to marine tourism and commercial fishing jobs when there is an oil spill. In their ad campaign, Enbridge trumpets the creation of 3,000 jobs at the peak of construction, but when Allan examined their report, she found that they are actually person-years of employment during construction, and the peak of construction only lasts three months. At best, Enbridge can claim 1,000 short-term construction jobs for the project. Allan says person-years of employment are often used interchangeably as jobs, but they are not jobs. They represent a full-time equivalent of one year of employment.

"Therefore one needs to divide by the life of the construction project — in this case four years. The figure should be presented as an annual average person-years of employment to better compare it to the commonly understood notion of jobs," Allan says. "After holding a position for 10 years, no one would ever say they had 10 jobs. However, this is how person years of employment are often presented in the Enbridge Application."

The Joint Review Panel held often-controversial public hearings across BC in 2012 and 2013. Five protesters were arrested after sneaking into the closed Vancouver hearing. In Victoria, spectators had to watch a live feed at a hotel three kilometres away. Enbridge stunned the hearings in Prince George on February 27th 2012 by saying "the scientific literature is clear" that species "inevitably recover" following an oil spill. It went on to suggest that oil spills "could generate economic spin-offs."

'TRUST ME' IS NOT GOOD ENOUGH

On May 31, 2013, after making an astonishing comeback to win the provincial election, British Columbia Premier Christy Clark rejected the Enbridge pipeline proposal. The government's 99-page final argument read "it is not clear from the evidence that [Enbridge] will in fact be able to respond effectively to spills from the pipeline itself, or from tankers transporting diluted bitumen from the proposed Kitimat terminal." Then, bluntly, 'trust me' is not good enough in this case." Environment minister Terry Lake did leave the door ajar by saying they couldn't support the pipeline "at this point" because of environmental concerns. But Lakes told an Alberta reporter there is still a "pathway to yes." BC has long stuck to demands for five conditions to be met to win approval for the project, among them: successful completion of the environmental review process, world-leading oil spill response systems both on land and on the water, addressing aboriginal and treaty rights and ensuring the province receives a fair share of the financial benefits. In early November 2013, Clark found the pathway. In Vancouver Clark and Premier Redford held a press conference to announce a "framework" that satisfied the five contentious conditions. The post-conference photo-op caught them walking with cheerful smiles on their faces and to-go coffee cups in their hands looking for all the world like colleagues returning to the office after a nice lunch.

In early November most of Canada was still transfixed on the scandal involving improper expenses accounting by three senators and the train wreck of the crack-smoking mayor of Toronto, Rob Ford, which garnered international attention. A perfect time at which to murmur news of an abrupt reversal on a campaign promise. On the campaign trail in 2012, Christy Clark had painted herself as the defender of virginal BC against invading oil interests from Alberta. In October of that year, Clark had a famously "frosty" meeting with Alberta Premier Alison Redford. Clark dug in her heels over a demand for what was vaguely described as British Columbia's "fair share." On November 5th, 2013, she shucked the shining armour and announced with her new chum Alison that they'd reached a tentative agreement on approval of the Northern Gateway. The breakthrough came when Clark dropped her deal-breaker demand for a share of Alberta's royalties. She even rephrased her sabre-rattling vague demand for a "fair share" of the profits from the Northern Gateway to a warm and fuzzy goal of "ensuring fair fiscal and economic benefits to both provinces." The rote phrasing of the joint press release reads eerily like a Stephen Harper PMO creation: "we are laying the foundation to work together to reach new markets, create jobs and strengthen both our economies, and Canada."

The coastal communities of BC need only look northward to see how much devastation an oil spill can wreak.

STILL-OILY ALASKA

Alaskans have been struggling to put their lives back in order ever since shortly after midnight on March 24, 1989, when the oil tanker Exxon

Valdez struck Bligh Reef in Prince William Sound, spilling more than 11 million gallons of crude oil. A Federal study done in 2011 estimates that 85 tons of crude are still poisoning the area 22 years later. At the Prince William Sound Science Center there are displays of jars of oil-stained sand and gooey black rocks still being dug up from the site of the spill. An American sociologist surveyed the tiny fishing village of Cordova, on the eastern side of Prince William Sound, five months after the catastrophe. He found shattered people suffering sleepless nights, unfocused anger, misplaced emotions, unwanted thoughts, lost friendships, and broken families. Bob van Brocklin, who was mayor at the time of the spill, committed suicide in 1993. His note said he killed himself partly because he was unable to help Cordova recover economically and emotionally from the crisis. Exxon has kept a generation of litigation lawyers in BMWs for 23 years fighting tooth and nail against a lawsuit brought by 32,000 fishermen, Alaska natives and landowners. More than 25 years on, the lawsuit is still dragging on and the lawyers are, presumably, buying more beemers. Alaska was tragically unlucky enough to be the nearest coastline when the Exxon Valdez slopped its load into the pristine Pacific. There is a magic place of ethereal natural beauty on the BC coast in the worst place possible: the path of the Northern Gateway pipeline.

SPIRIT BEARS, FISHING WOLVES AND THE LAST RAINFOREST

Just shy of the coast going west along the proposed pipeline route, the boreal forest changes radically: the skinny birch, larch and pine give way to the massive, ancient Douglas Fir, Red Cedar and Sitka Spruce of the Great Bear Rainforest. The air becomes very humid, rain falls constantly and moss drapes the trees in long, bushy clumps. Some of the trees in the

Great Bear are 1,500 years old – mere saplings when the Roman Empire was collapsing. The Great Bear is home to two extraordinary animal species that are unique in the world. Spirit bears are a subspecies of black bears that are ghostly white from a genetic anomaly. The last 200 spirit bears on the planet live in and around the Great Bear. The survival of the forest depends on the bears and vice versa. The bears carpet the forest floor with salmon carcasses, providing vital nutrition to the trees. In return, the tree roots and canopies prevent soil erosion and landslides that would ruin the salmon streams that feed the bears.

Another astonishing sub-species is salmon-hunting coastal wolves. The wolf packs swim up to 10 kilometres among the islands off the coast hunting salmon. Enbridge says the pipeline won't cross the Great Bear Rainforest, but Darcy Dobell, vice president of the Pacific region of the World Wildlife Fund, says the WWF uses an eco-regional boundary, rather than an administrative one, to define the Great Bear. So, the rivers and streams in these watersheds, together with the rainforest, coastal zone and ocean comprise a single living system.

THE WAR IN THE WOODS

In spring 2013, residents of Sonora Island in the Great Bear found out that TimberWest Corp., which has long been known as the conservation laggard among the major loggers in the region, was preparing to legally clear cut some of the last old-growth stands on the island. The Timber-West tenure is located in the least protected portion of the area and among the hardest hit by logging, with most of the Rainforest already reduced to second-growth forest. The stands slated for logging include 700-year old Douglas Fir and Western Red Cedar. Under TimberWest's interpretation of logging regulations, they claim that the patches they plan to log are second growth despite the obvious presence of giant trees and the community's carefully compiled records, which identify significant old-growth stands.

The environmentalists and the loggers have been negotiating since the end of the so-called War in the Woods of the 1990s. The 'war' was sparked in the early 1980s by a rising tide of public concern about industrial logging in Clayoquot Sound on the west coast of Vancouver Island. The culmination came in the huge protests, logging road blockades and mass arrests of the 1993 "Clayoquot Summer." Today, the impasse centres on how to meet the target of preserving 70 per cent of the Rainforest's old growth while still harvesting 2.7 million cubic metres of logs a year.

THE CALCULUS OF CARBON

One challenge to creating a sustainable economy is how to balance ecological with economic objectives. Carbon offsets place a dollar value on carbon and contribute to this balancing act by displacing, or offsetting, carbon created by burning fossil fuel. The carbon product can then be bought by a person or company to counteract the carbon emissions they are unable to reduce. An energy company could 'buy' the equivalent in carbon they emit and earmark it for land conservation projects or renewables elsewhere such as tree planting or solar energy programs. The carbon released by deforestation, like that in the Great Bear, is another issue. Dr. James Tansey is an associate professor at the University of British Columbia and co-founder and CEO of a carbon-offset company called Offsetters in Vancouver. In a May 2013 op-ed piece for the Vancouver Sun, Dr. Tansey wrote, "[global] deforestation results in around eight gigatonnes of emissions of carbon dioxide per year, more than 10 times the total emissions of Canada." Tansey said the biggest opportunity to decrease emissions is investing in projects "that reduce emissions from deforestation and degradation (REDD). Projects in Indonesia, Brazil and the Congo have already demonstrated that forest areas can be protected from harvest activities, which prevents the carbon they store from moving into the atmosphere." The business model for such projects is simple; offset sales pay landowners to forego income from deforestation, so trees that would be cleared are allowed to stand and continue to store their carbon.

THE ECONOMICS OF LIVE BEARS

The Victoria-based Centre for Integral Economics is an independent think tank that studies how to reconcile economics, social justice and environmental issues. In 2003, the centre did an analysis of the revenues derived from British Columbia's grizzly bears. They found that grizzly bear-viewing ecotourism is conservatively worth $6.1 million annually in BC, while the grizzly hunt brings in only half as much. The worldwide market for eco-adventure tourism in 2010 was estimated at $89 billion, with 10 per cent annual growth. Kevin Smith, president of an eco-tourism company, identified in an op-ed piece some practical reasons why bear viewing and bear shooting will never coexist: both obviously need to operate in bear country, but where bears are shot, "bear viewing is bad, because the bears hide. No bear-viewing business can prosper there because, like all businesses, tourism needs a degree of certainty to survive." Smith identifies the obvious perils of shooting photos in an area where hunters are shooting—and sometimes only wounding—fully grown grizzlies.

WALKING THE LINE

On The Line is a 2011 documentary by filmmakers Frank Wolf and Todd McGowan of their trip on foot, bike, raft and kayak along the 2,400 kilometres of the proposed pipeline route. In BC, they meet a fishing guide on the Stikine River who talks about how a leak on his river would put him and all the other guides on the river out of work permanently and questions whether the part-time jobs that would be created building the pipeline are worth it. One First Nations man standing by a rushing BC river, questions the wisdom of "blindly going into a project like Enbridge and gambling with something like this," as he gestures to the river. They hear from a fishing boat captain that the second highest wave ever recorded thundered down Hecate Strait, where Douglas Channel meets the Pacific. Master Mariner Mal Walsh has over 40 years of experience in international oil exploration and shipping and is concerned that the Enbridge tanker routes pose a serious risk to the BC coast. "The Enbridge tanker transport proposal, in its current form, represents too great a risk to a remote and still pristine area of BC's Central Coast, a region of this coast that is exposed to the most severe winter weather conditions," Walsh said. Kitimat-born journalist Robin Rowland uncovered a report by the Geological Survey of Canada and the Department of Fisheries and Oceans that warned of a tsunami hazard and a possible seismic fault in the Douglas Channel. Rowland reported that in October 1974, a giant underwater landslide on Douglas Channel near Kitimat triggered a three-metre tsunami. Six months later, a second earthquake caused an eight-metre tsunami.

After meandering west over the prairie, the pipeline slams into the immense graniteness of the Rocky Mountains where two tunnels will have to be bored, drilled and blasted six-and-a-half kilometres through the mountains between Smithers and Terrace, the pipeline's most volatile terrain. The Kitimat Ranges, part of the coast mountain range, are rippled with steep, narrow valleys down which powerful landslides thundered in 1978 and 1992. In the last 40 years, large landslides have severed a natural gas pipeline in the nearby Bulkley Range three times. Smithers-based geomorphologist Jim Schwab told Northword Magazine, "The unstable mountainous terrain across west-central BC is not a safe location for pipelines. Eventually a landslide will sever a pipeline."

GOOD TO GO

The Joint Review Panel conducting the review of the Northern Gateway pipeline gave its approval in December 2013, subject to 209 conditions such as oil-spill response speed, restrictions on foreign workers and mandated minimums on hiring First Nations for construction. The approval came as no surprise to opponents and commentators. The government is expected to make its decision about the Northern Gateway pipeline by June 19 2014. If approval is given, construction on the pipeline could begin in 2014 and bitumen could be flowing by 2018.

ENERGY EAST

On August 2, 2013, TransCanada Pipelines, the proponents of the Keystone XL pipeline from Alberta to Texas, submitted a proposal to pipe Alberta crude to New Brunswick. The $12 billion Energy East TransCanada pipeline project would convert about 3,000 kilometres of their existing natural gas main line to ship oil from Alberta to its terminus in Quebec. From there, about 1,400 kilometres of new pipe would be built to Saint John, New Brunswick for processing at Irving Oil's massive refinery or be shipped offshore. The company hopes to complete construction to Quebec City by late 2017 and to Saint John in 2018. Environmentalists are gearing up to battle Energy East as hard as they have fought the Keystone XL and Northern Gateway. But of the three proposals to get Alberta crude to tidewater and the export market, on the surface, Energy East would appear to make the most sense for a number of reasons: most of the pipeline is already in place so there is no need to lay much more. There is no need to drill right through a Rocky Mountain. And there is massive refining capacity ready to go. Building the new pipeline stretch to Saint John would create well-paying but temporary construction jobs and most of the value-added refining jobs would remain in Canada instead of being exported to the US. But, former CIBC chief economist Jeff Rubin says Energy East is not the silver bullet the industry paints it to be. Proponents of the pipeline claim Energy East is in the national interest because it lessens our reliance on foreign oil and would reduce the price of gas. But sky-high extraction costs make Alberta crude among the most expensive sources of oil in the world, which roughly equates it to the high price of imported oil. That means drivers will still pay the same price at the pump. While the cheaper gas is a popular selling point for pipelines, the reality is the savings of a few cents can be tripled with slower speeds and proper vehicle maintenance — mundane topics until we consider lower speeds would reduce accidents and vehicle maintenance would also create jobs. Rubin says the only benefits of the pipeline will go, as usual, to the oil sands players. "The Irving family, who are building the export terminal in St. John, also get a check mark. New Brunswick, as well, will gladly take the boost from the economic activity," Rubin says. "Only Ottawa and, of course, Alberta, will see a ton of cash." Rubin asks rhetorically about the cost of driving up production from the oil sands. "Should we at least consider taking a few deep breaths before plunging ahead with loading more rail cars with oil and building more pipelines? Nature put that oil in the ground. Until we better understand the ramifications of taking it out, maybe we should think about leaving it there for a while longer." The project is in

Trevor Greene and Mike Velemirovich

limbo, with government officials giving the familiar refrain that 'there has been inadequate consultation with First Nations communities and the proposed route poses unacceptable risk to ground water.'

A KITCHEN TABLE CHAT

Dave Core, a farmer, landowner and expert on pipeline regulation, addressed the Senate Energy Committee in February 2013. Core told the assembled Senators that the National Energy Board [NEB], which held the hearings on the Northern Gateway pipeline, is not independent and unbiased but "protects the interests of pipeline companies." Core talked about the hundreds of oil pipeline spills that had not been cleaned up in Ontario, Manitoba and the Northwest Territories. He said it is illegal for pipeline companies to abandon their corroded steel pipes in the ground, which is a hazard to groundwater and livestock. Core showed how the NEB hasn't prosecuted billions of dollars in abandonment liabilities on 70,000 kilometres of federally regulated pipelines.

Core's testimony was heartfelt and compelling:

"... I would like you to pretend you are sitting around a kitchen table with your family and a 'land agent' has just left you with a brown envelope with a Section 87 Notice, an NEB Regulatory Notice, stating that a pipeline company is going to put a pipeline in your backyard and the easement agreement and the compensation offer are included.

The stress has only just begun. Next come teams of land agents, the men trained in profiling and in telling every tale they can to get the deal signed while they sit at your kitchen table drinking your coffee. He/she might even be your neighbour's son or daughter. It is like you have stepped into a spaghetti western with cowboys coming to your door, not packing a gun, but a big smile, lots of lies and packing government regulations that allow them to threaten you if you question them.

Landowners are not just stakeholders. Like you, Honourable Senators, we are property owners. We bought our property as a place to live, a lifestyle choice, an investment, to ranch our cattle, to farm or run any other business zoning allowed. We did not request pipelines. We live, raise families and work on these properties, yet we have had pipelines enforced on our backyards that do not respect our stewardship or legal obligations. Our name is on the title and the NEB legislation leaves our future to the whim of pipeline companies and their regulatory partners."

Core described how under the May 2012 Omnibus Bill, NEB regulations were changed to penalize farmers who do not ask permission to cross pipelines with a maximum fine of up to $1,000,000 and/or imprisonment up to five years. "Too bad the presidents of the pipeline companies do not suffer the same consequences for polluting miles of private property. Instead they get multimillion-dollar pensions," Core said.

AN INCONVENIENT SANDBAR

The federal government has taken great pains to show that the Northern Gateway is going to be both an economic and environmental success. One of the biggest concerns is an oil spill in the waters around Vancouver. Natural Resources Minister Joe Oliver held a press conference on March 21st 2013 to trumpet Canada's oil spill defenses. All the media duly gathered by Vancouver Harbour with a beautiful photo-op view of the North Shore Mountains. The scene was all set for BC's largest oil spill response vessel to drift into view behind Oliver. But the 30-ton *M.J. Green,* Western Canada Marine Response Corporation's largest spill-response vessel, was just then stuck on a sandbar that it had ploughed into off the mouth of the Fraser River enroute from its base on Vancouver Island to the press conference. A Canadian Auto Workers spokesman was astonished that "... the safety and protection of Canada's busiest port is dependent on a quick response in the event of an oil spill and this is what we get — a response vessel grounding itself and taking 11 hours to arrive in Vancouver."

THE DILEMMA OF DILBIT

Unrefined oil sands are properly called bitumen. Bitumen is junk energy. Every joule, or unit of energy, invested in extracting and processing bitumen yields only four to six joules in the form of crude oil. Conventional oil production in North America, by contrast, yields about 15 joules. Raw dilbit has the consistency of peanut butter and can't flow through a pipeline, forcing oil companies to dilute it with a mix of toxic chemicals known as condensate to make it fluid enough to flow in the pipeline. Condensate contains poisonous chemicals like benzene, toluene and hydrogen sulphide. In a spill, the condensate evaporates, releasing an extremely dangerous toxic cloud. The thick tar that is left sinks to the bottom, coating the river or ocean bottom. Conventional oil spills, like in the Gulf of Mexico or Alaska, are cleaned up with surface booms and skimmers that catch only a small percentage of the oil spilled. The emergency plan Enbridge submitted to the federal review panel in August 2012 only addressed spills of conventional crude oil. Enbridge was quoted in the August 26th 2012 Globe and Mail that conventional oil and dilbit "react the same way once spilled." Department of Fisheries and Oceans scientist Kenneth Lee emphatically begs to differ. Lee, the head of DFO's Centre for Offshore Oil Gas and Energy Research, said, " ... the Northern Gateway pipeline proposal lacks key information on the chemical composition of the reference oils used in the hypothetical spill models."

CULTURE OF DEVIANCE

In the past decade, Enbridge has glopped an embarrassing hundreds of thousands of barrels of oil from hundreds of spills and leaks without much attention or controversy. But the Kalamazoo River spill not only killed the river, it wounded the people living peacefully on the riverbank. Evaporating toxic condensate from the bitumen made hundreds of people sick and coated more than 50 kilometres of the river bottom with tar. Incredibly, as of July 2012, no Enbridge executive or employee had been reprimanded or punished for his or her role in the costliest inland pipeline spill in U.S. history. Far from contrite, just a few months later, Enbridge's 12 board members voted to raise their annual retainers by $30,000 and jacked up the salary of CEO and president, Patrick Daniel, to $8.1 million. CEO bonuses generally dwarf salaries. In its report on Kalamazoo, the U.S. National Transportation Safety Board (NTSB) wrote that Enbridge had a "culture of deviance" on safety matters. A BC-based engineering firm says the amount of energy needed to produce tar sands energy might not be worth the effort and environmental risk. It's called Energy Return On Investment (EROI) and refers to the amount of energy that must be expended in order to produce more energy. C.J. Peter Associates found that getting oil sands bitumen from Alberta to China requires so much energy for such scant EROI it might not be worth the effort. In testifying at public hearings in Prince George in January 2012, the firm's Norman Jacob used a chilling analogy for the dilemma: "when animals expend more energy foraging than they obtain from plant food sources they die. Societies that ignore EROI necessarily fail."

IT'S WHEN, NOT IF

Over a 30-day period in March and April 2012, there were 13 oil spills around the world, mostly in North America. An Environment Canada report says that "based on current levels of tanker traffic, Canada can expect over 100 small oil spills, about 10 moderate spills and at least one major spill off-shore each year. A catastrophic spill (over 10,000 tonnes) may occur once every 15 years." The Vancouver Sun's Stephen Hume wrote a column on oil spills in June 2012. He said, " … [his] reporting career … was ushered in by a series of massive pipeline spills in Alberta more than 40 years ago. The pipeline industry has had almost half a century to work on the problem, yet oil spills, explosions, fires and toxic pollution as a consequence of ruptures are anything but exceptional. They still happen on an almost daily basis." Over the past decade or so in the greater Vancouver area, hundreds of thousands of litres of toxic fuel has soaked into the ground or spread across the ocean.

Forget the Northern Gateway. The southern BC coast has another, older pipeline bogey to fear. The Kinder Morgan Pipeline carries oil from Edmonton to its marine terminal in Burnaby, east of Vancouver proper. From there, its tankers negotiate the shallow approaches to Vancouver Harbour to the Georgia Strait and on to the Strait of Juan de Fuca. Kinder Morgan is the biggest pipeline company in the US. Richard Kinder was Enron's president until 1996. Kinder is the 110th richest man alive with a net worth of $8.2 billion. For the record, it's Kinder as in "kindergarten" not as in "kinder, gentler." Like Enbridge, Kinder Morgan seems to be extremely laid back about safety. They have had 44 accidents over the last two years. Every day, two million barrels of gasoline and jet and diesel fuel, and 13.5 billion cubic feet of natural gas move through Kinder Morgan's 35,000 miles of pipelines in the U.S.

MOTHER OCEAN AS GARBAGE CAN

In 2008, a federal judge fined a Kinder Morgan subsidiary $240,000 for violating ocean dumping laws in 2003 when a company supervisor hired a ship to insert 160 tonnes of potassium chloride into the Pacific Ocean. That pitifully miniscule amount of money is barely a rounding error for a multibillion-dollar entity like Kinder Morgan and is undoubtedly a scant deterrent. An agent for the U.S. Environmental Protection Agency said, "it's hard to imagine a clearer violation of the Ocean Dumping Act. Intentionally using the ocean as a garbage can … is not only morally wrong, it's a crime." The Wilderness Committee, a nonprofit based in Vancouver, has tracked Kinder Morgan's woes; on July 24, 2007 when a construction crew inadvertently hit an unmarked pipe in Burnaby with an excavator, 250,000 litres of oil shot out of the ground, soaking a residential neighbourhood and seeping into the nearby Burrard Inlet. At least 50 homes had to be evacuated. A pipeline rupture on January 24th 2012 at the Sumas Mountain tank farm spilled about 110,000 litres of oil. Local residents reported health problems including nausea, headaches and fatigue, and schoolchildren were kept indoors for fear of airborne toxins.

Trevor Greene and Mike Velemirovich

GOOD AND BAD SCIENCE

HOW SMOG CLEARED THE AIR

Smog, short for smoky fog, was first recognized as a problem in California in 1943 when the Los Angeles Times reported a "gas attack" of pollution that stung eyes, scratched throats and reduced visibility to just a few blocks. California's population is roughly equal to Canada. Most Californians are squeezed into a valley region roughly the size of Nova Scotia. So put tens of millions of people in a valley, add a passion for cars then mix in warm, moist air from the Pacific Ocean and you have a situation that created the California Air Resources Board in 1967. Who was the tree hugging, hippie governor who created such a powerful legislative body, you ask? It was — wait for it — Ronald Reagan. But he simply did what any smart politician would do with millions of voters demanding action on brown air filled with nitrogen oxides and particulates. He gave the people — he gave the *voters* — what they wanted: cleaner air. A few years later in 1970, as pollution concerns increased across the US, the EPA, or Environmental Protection Agency, was formed. The EPA is a federal agency mandated to regulate air quality in the US. Such a massive federal agency with a sweeping liberal mandate must have been created by a tree hugging, hippie president, right? No, it was Richard Nixon. Turns out tricky Dick was simply responding to the millions of voters from coast to coast that were demanding environmental action.

Following the 1973 Arab oil crisis, the US Congress introduced Corporate Average Fuel Economy [CAFE] standards in 1975, as a way to improve fuel economy and decrease American dependence on foreign oil. CAFE standards examine the average fuel efficiency of auto manufacturers. CAFE standards took effect in 1978 and between then and 1984, the auto industry improved overall efficiency from 18 miles per gallon to 27 mpg; a whopping 50 per cent improvement in just six years. Efficiency levels lingered at 27 mpg for over 25 years. As late as 2007 I [Mike] sat in meetings where boardrooms of auto industry executives agreed that hybrid cars were just a fad and that internal combustion engines were as good as they could be without making further improvements prohibitively expensive. It took newly elected President Obama to give a jolt to CAFE standards. Many auto manufacturers now offer plug-in electric cars that operate on pure electricity and can even be recharged at home using solar panels. I now sit in meetings with auto executives who proudly point to retail launch dates for cars like the Volkswagen XL1 that can achieve 282 mpg. The excitement with which these hardened auto executives describe impending clean technology reveals a little-known, but promising fact: most people inside the auto industry are closet environmentalists. Personally they want to work on projects that improve efficiency and lessen the impact of cars on our world, but they have their careers in the fossil-fuel industry to protect. Closet environmentalists in the fossil-fuel industry are not confined to carmakers. At a posh Utah ski resort in 2008 I delivered a talk to the Society of Independent Gasoline Marketers of America. The audience of just a few dozen people owned over 30,000 gas stations across the United States and I was there to present the environmental opportunities of diesel fuel. "Environmental opportunities in the fuel business" is code for "you're going to sell less fuel." I anticipated a tough audience but I was pleasantly surprised that I was dead

Trevor Greene and Mike Velemirovich

wrong. Many people in the crowd were second- or third-generation owners who later told me they fully recognized the world is changing and for the sake of their children, they knew we have to do something and they wanted to participate. My toughest audience turned out to be the most promising. The challenge is that corporations are hard-wired to make as much money as possible without breaking the law. Despite the best intentions of employees who want to make a difference, corporations cannot risk wasting money on clean technology for fear others will steal their market share. This is where astute government legislation can level the playing field to allow all companies to pursue greentech at the same time without sacrificing market share. It requires political leaders with vision and strength of character like Ronald Reagan and Richard Nixon and now Barack Obama, who significantly strengthened CAFE standards for the first time in a generation. Political vision, strength of character and most importantly, trust in science seems to be glaringly absent north of the border.

BAD SCIENCE

The Northern Gateway pipeline will be judged on science "not simply on political criteria," Prime Minister Harper said on August 7th, 2012. But by August 19th, 2012, pink slips had magically appeared on the desks of 92 habitat staff in the BC Fisheries and Oceans department (DFO). The department was halved from levels 10 years ago. The cuts took out the offices in Prince George and Smithers that would have had the lead in reporting on pipeline spills. The division that would have been called in if there was a spill disappeared entirely. The ravishing of the DFO offices wasn't the government's first arbitrary science smack-down. In October 2012, the Polar Environment Atmospheric Research Laboratory (PEARL) packed up its igloo. The PEARL was established in Eureka, Nunavut in 1993 under the

Mulroney government's progressive Green Plan. It is about 1,000 kilometres from the North Pole on Ellesmere Island and was built to monitor, study and report on the status of the Earth's protective Arctic ozone layer. The government shut it down in April 2012.

A MASSACRE OF KNOWLEDGE

Scientists are calling it "libricide." Seven of the nine world-famous Department of Fisheries and Oceans (DFO) libraries were closed by autumn 2013, ostensibly to digitize the materials and reduce costs. But sources told the independent Tyee in December that only a fraction of the 600,000-volume collection had been digitized. And, a secret federal document notes that a paltry $443,000 a year will be saved. The massacre was done quickly, with no record keeping and no attempt to preserve the material in universities. Scientists said precious collections were consigned to dumpsters, were burned or went to landfills. Probably the most famous facility to get the ax is the library of the venerable St. Andrews Biological Station in St. Andrews, New Brunswick, which environmental scientist Rachel Carson used extensively to research her seminal book on toxins, *Silent Spring*. The government had just spent millions modernizing the facility. Also closed were the Freshwater Institute library in Winnipeg and the library of the Northwest Atlantic Fisheries Centre in St. John's, Newfoundland, both world-class collections. Hundreds of years of carefully compiled research into aquatic systems, fish stocks and fisheries from the 1800s and early 1900s went into the bin or up in smoke. Irreplaceable documents like the 50 volumes produced by the H.M.S. Challenger expedition of the late 1800s that discovered thousands of new sea creatures, are now moldering in landfills. Renowned Dalhousie University biologist Jeff Hutchings calls the closures "an assault on civil society. It is always unnerving from a research and scientist perspective to watch a government undermine basic research. Losing libraries is not a neutral act," Hutchings says. He blames political convictions for the knowledge massacre. "It must be about ideology. Nothing else fits," said Hutchings. "What that ideology is, is not clear. Does it reflect that part of the Harper government that doesn't think government should be involved in the very things that affect our lives? Or is it that the role of government is not to collect books or fund science?" Hutchings said the closures fit into a larger pattern of "fear and insecurity" within the Harper government, "about how to deal with science and knowledge."

THE DEATH OF A LIVING LABORATORY

The Experimental Lakes Area (ELA) is a series of 58 lakes in Northwestern Ontario that is considered to be one of the world's most important aquatic research areas. Since 1968, the ELA has gained an international reputation for research into everything from acid rain to climate change to fish farming. In May 2012, the DFO announced that the facility would be closed at the end of the fiscal year, March 2013. It claimed that the kind of research the ELA was carrying out was "better suited to universities." According to Maude Barlow, head of the Council of Canadians and a former senior adviser on water to the UN General Assembly, "the (ELT) is a world-class, living, outdoor laboratory where scientists have studied how to protect freshwater for decades. The federal government is shaming Canadians in the eyes of the world and killing a major gift to water science at the very moment we are really beginning to understand the depth of the global water crisis." The closing sparked outrage from around the world. Swedish ecologist Ragnar Elmgren called the closing of the ELA "an act of wanton destruction of the scientific value." Elmgren raged that the trashing of the ELA is "the kind of act one expects from the Taliban in Afghanistan, not from the government of a civilized and educated nation." Harvard University aquatic sciences professor Elsie Sunderland told the Winnipeg Free Press that she was shocked. "This is one of the foremost research projects and places to do research in the world. To have it shut down is just appalling. It's just embarrassing." Near the end of April 2013 the Ontario government came riding to the rescue, announcing it would collaborate with the government of Manitoba to keep the ELA in operation.

THE SCIENTIST VS THE POLITICIAN

Dr. James Hansen is the leading climate scientist in the US. He retired in April 2013 after 32 years heading up NASA's Goddard Institute for Space Studies. Hansen introduced climate change to the global lexicon while testifying before the US Congress on a boiling June day in 1988. With one sentence Hansen defined the ultimate challenge of the modern age: "it is time to stop waffling so much and say that the evidence is pretty strong that the greenhouse effect is here." During a stop in Washington D.C. in late April to shore up support for the Keystone pipeline, Natural Resources Minister Joe Oliver said Hansen was "crying wolf" with his "exaggerated" opinions on Keystone XL. The CBC quoted Matthias Schneider, a German climate researcher "if Canada proceeds [with development of the tar sands], and we do nothing, it will be game over for the climate." Oliver thought "[the statement] is exaggerated rhetoric. It's frankly nonsense. I don't know why he said it, but he should be ashamed of having said it." Hansen, one of Time magazine's most influential people of 2006, fired back shortly afterwards; "the current government is a Neanderthal government on this issue, but Canada can actually be a leader," he said. "I have hopes that Canada will actually be a good example for the United States but the present government is certainly not." Dr. Hansen didn't mince words: "They're in the hip pocket of the fossil fuel industry, as you can see, but that doesn't mean that the Canadian people are." Hansen told the Times that he would use his extra time and energy to bring more lawsuits against the federal and state governments over their failure to limit emissions.

Trevor Greene and Mike Velemirovich

PATHOLOGICAL GOVERNANCE

"A nation of sheep begets a government of wolves"
- Edward R. Murrow

Dr. Warren Bell, a British Columbia GP, addressed the Joint Review Panel hearings on the Enbridge pipeline on January 28th 2013. Bell, who has training in psychology, said the toxic Enbridge controversy is a symptom of "structural pathology" at the heart of Canada's government. He traces it back to the first Europeans who through a "combination of force of arms, disease, mass immigration and various legalistic arrangements — including a genocidal strategy called the residential school system — relentlessly marginalized our First Nations and irreparably destroyed their intimate connection to the ecosystem." Bell points out that hundreds of First Nations communities are squarely in the pipeline route. The second pathological element is our much-maligned electoral system. Our first-past-the-post system is "psychologically grossly inefficient. Especially in complex or conflictual situations, it generates a mixture of cynicism, despair and anger." The third element, the all-powerful Prime Minister's Office, is "an invitation to social disaster. The illusion of efficiency in political decision-making is subverted by the opportunity for hard line autocracy," Bell suggests. The final element is the surge in corporate influence that absolves employees of personal responsibility for often-disastrous decisions and puts profit above all else. Bell describes a patient in his mid-twenties who said he was deeply depressed and anxious "about the overheated, depleted future he was heading towards. He felt that the government in this country was acting now to make it worse for him and his young children later."

Bell co-founded the Canadian Association of Physicians for the Environment [CAPE] in 1995, which scientifically examines the intimate inter-relationship between human and ecosystem health. Bell discusses Stephen Harper's autocratic ways, and his "willingness to mask his own renowned intensity behind a rigidly bland persona is a truer indication of his deep commitment to power." The doctor's fourfold cure is nothing new: repairing the relationship with our First Nations, electoral reform, loosening the iron grip of the PMO and reining in the overwhelming power and influence of the corporate sector. "Until we do these four things, our country is vulnerable to political, social and ecological upheaval that will retard our development as a nation, and likely offer ruin to the lives of future generations."

The renowned filmmaker Bonnie Klein was part of a wave of over 200,000 Vietnam War-era women and men who immigrated to Canada from the United States out of opposition to the war. Her children, Naomi and Seth are noted social activists. Bonnie Klein received the Order of Canada in May 2013 and made an impassioned speech lamenting the direction her adopted country has taken: "rather than protect our precious resources; our land, water, air and our own health from climate disaster, we are shaming dissenting individuals and groups by labeling them naive or subversive. We are allowing partisan interests to silence our scientists and civil servants."

SHUSHED LIBRARIANS

The Vancouver Sun reported in March 2013 that a new code of conduct at Library and Archives Canada [LAC] dictated that federal librarians and archivists who visit classrooms, attend conferences or speak up at public

Trevor Greene and Mike Velemirovich

meetings on their own time are engaging in "high risk" activities. Staff has to clear such "personal" activities with their managers in advance to ensure there are no conflicts or "other risks to LAC." The *Library and Archives Canada's Code of Conduct: Values and Ethics* came into effect in January 2013 and dictates that employees have a "duty of loyalty" to the "duly elected government." Toni Samek, a professor of library and information studies at the University of Alberta told the Sun "once you start picking on librarians and archivists, it's pretty sad." Samek characterised several clauses in the Code as "severe" and "outrageous." Our archivists are top-notch and often invited to lecture internationally — apparently not for much longer: "On occasion, LAC employees may be asked by third parties to teach or to speak at or be a guest at conferences as a personal activity or part-time employment. Such activities have been identified as high risk to LAC and to the employee with regard to conflict of interest, conflict of duties and duty of loyalty." The wording wouldn't be out of place in an internal memo in China or North Korea: "As public servants, our duty of loyalty to the Government of Canada and its elected officials extends beyond our workplace to our personal activities," the Code says, adding that public servants "must maintain awareness of their surroundings, their audience and how their words or actions could be interpreted (or misinterpreted)."

PARANOID BUREAUCRACY

Natural Resources Minister Joe Oliver got his first tirade of 2013 off early. In the second week of January, Oliver fiercely labeled the many environmentalists opposed to the Northern Gateway pipeline as being funded by "billionaire socialists from the United States who are trying to undermine the Canadian economy." Oliver suggested, "[the American billionaire socialists'] goal is to stop any major project no matter what the cost to Canadian families in lost jobs and economic growth. No forestry. No mining. No oil. No gas. No more hydro-electric dams." He singled out billionaire philanthropist George Soros, who gave away over $8 billion to human rights, public health, and education causes between 1979 and 2011. Toronto Star columnist David Olive weighed in on January 2013: "our prime minister trembles with unseemly rage that the likes of Leonardo DiCaprio may voice an objection to projects that will have a multi-generational, and irrevocable, impact on nature and social conditions in hundreds of communities across North America."

AN INCONVENIENT ARTIST

Environmental artist Franke James is a Toronto visual artist, storyteller and environmental advocate. She was flabbergasted when her carefully planned 20-city tour of Europe in 2011 was abruptly cancelled. James' *What Can One Person Do, When 6.8 Billion Are Frying The Planet?* is an irreverent series of colourful graphics about the challenges we are facing from climate change. Her *"Dear Prime Minister"* graphic essay asked why the Prime Minister is asking Canadians to choose between the economy and the environment. "It's as if Stephen Harper were the CEO of Canada the corporation and we were his employees and we were not allowed to step out of line or say what we believe is right or true because that would upset the company's brand." Her European tour was cancelled in July 2011 by Foreign Affairs. A media monitoring report at the time from the same bureaucrats listed James as "an inconvenient artist." She was ninth on a list that included the assassination of the mayor of Kandahar by a suicide bomber. James told the Toronto Star it is "chilling and shocking" to be "painted as persona non grata" abroad by the federal government. "To be on the list of hot foreign issues, it was just shocking," James said in an interview. "I'm right up there with

Arctic sovereignty and Afghanistan." Undaunted and defiant, James held a crowd-funded, outdoor art show, *Banned on the Hill* in downtown Ottawa on November 2nd, 2011. The Guardian's Suzanne Goldenberg picked up on the story and chronicled a farcical tale of paranoia and a document trail across seven government departments. "Harper's personal communications team followed her on Twitter. Senior civil servants signed off on emails discussing her." It wasn't the first case of bureaucratic gridlock: government bureaucrats exchanged more than 50 different emails in March 2012 discussing whether to grant an interview to an Ottawa Citizen reporter on a National Research Council study on snowfall patterns—and then turned him down.

SILENCED SCIENTISTS

Macleans wrote a piece in May 2013 titled "When Science Goes Silent." The article led with an example of a DFO scientist who did an interview with *Canada AM*; "the kind of innocuous and totally apolitical media commentary the man used to deliver 30 times or more each year." He did the interview after not hearing back from the PR department but wasn't concerned because he'd given many such interviews in the past and had even been named the DFO's spokesperson of the year. The article describes how "soon after arriving at his offices, the scientist was called before his regional director and given a formal verbal reprimand: talk to the media again without the explicit permission of the minister's office, he was warned, and there would be serious consequences — like a suspension without pay, or even dismissal."

The New York Times editorial board, arguably the most influential media group in the world, took the Harper government to task in a sharply worded editorial on September 21st 2013 that claimed the government was muzzling scientists. It drew an uncomfortable comparison to the right wing regime that invented a war in Iraq; "there was trouble of this kind here in the George W. Bush years, when scientists were asked to toe the party line on climate policy and endangered species. But nothing came close to what is being done in Canada." The editors characterized the arm lock on scientists as "an attempt to guarantee public ignorance." The piece closed strongly; "to all the other kinds of pollution the tar sands will yield, we must now add another: the degradation of vital streams of research and information."

MORE BANG FOR THE GREEN BUCK

The Bluegreen Alliance is composed of 14 of the largest unions and environmental organizations in Canada. The 15 million-strong organization advocates for the growth in the number and quality of jobs in the green economy. In November 2012 the Alliance published a report titled *More Bang for our Buck* that said the government could create 18,000 jobs if it junked tax incentives for oil and gas companies, and put the money in sustainable industries. The report, which was co-signed by the continent's largest union, the United Steelworkers, is based on past studies about the economic benefits of investments in emerging energy sectors such as wind and solar power. "The oil industry's plan to dramatically increase oil production will lead Canada in the wrong direction if we want to reduce pollution, ensure a healthy planet for our children and take advantage of the financial benefits of the renewable energy sector," it read. "While jobs will be created through oil sands expansion, the pace of development, as well as the location and type of jobs created, are not in the best interests of Canadian workers."

HUMAN RESOURCES MANAGEMENT BY MAIL
David McLaughlin and 30 of his colleagues on the National Round Table on the Environment and the Economy (NRTEE) learned of their demise on May 14th 2012 though the media and social websites. Foreign Affairs Minister John Baird bluntly explained the NRTEE's disbandment in the House;

"why should taxpayers have to pay for more than 10 reports promoting a carbon tax, something that the people of Canada have repeatedly rejected?" Alberta MP Bob Mills, who was his party's environment critic when Stephen Harper was opposition leader, reacted to the news by telling the House of Commons " … if you're smart you surround yourself with really smart people. And if you're dumb, you surround yourself with a bunch of cheerleaders. We don't need cheerleaders. What we need are smart people," Mills said. A courier eventually delivered an envelope to McLaughlin from Environment Canada that confirmed the decision to axe the NRTEE. Environment Minister Peter Kent said he decided to disband the Round Table to save money. Kent also suggested that he could get the same analysis and research from the Internet and from other unnamed sources. The Round Table's annual budget was $5.2 million. By comparison, the government approved $4.5 million for War of 1812 advertising that year. In August 2012, McLaughlin spoke to Postmedia News about the symbiosis of the economy and the environment in Canada. McLaughlin said he banged that drum for years. "If we say we are an energy superpower and we want to be an energy superpower, we have to be an environmental superpower too. We can't be an energy superpower and an environmental middle power. You've got to do the two together and find a way to do that." In autumn 2012, The Canadian Environmental Network suffered the same fate when Environment Canada pulled the lion's share of its funding. The Network linked small environmental groups across Canada to the federal government, which would ask the network for policy advice on local issues. The organization would then co-ordinate discussions between various smaller groups nationwide. "It was a real kick in the pants," said co-ordinator Dan Casselman. "If they'd given us some warning we might have had time to find money somewhere else." Like the NRTEE, the Canadian Environmental Network learned about its dissolution from Canada Post.

FROM THE MOUTHS OF BABES

Fifteen-year old Zoe Craig and Rekha Dhillon-Richardson, 13, lectured Canada on its poor record on climate change to the United Nations Committee on the Rights of the Child in September 2012. Zoe, a member of BC's Musqueam Nation, took a page out of ecologist, Sandra Steingraber's *Raising Elijah*, in asking the Committee to treat climate change as a critical threat to children and said children must have input into Canadian climate change policies. "My inherent right to life, and my right to culture as an indigenous person, are being jeopardized not only by climate change but by my country's lack of environmental standards and policies," she said. "Canada must give children a say in environmental policy." Rekha Dhillon-Richardson told the Committee that she is aghast by the failure of her government: "As a 13 year-old girl, I can understand why children's rights are needed, because they apply to me and others I know," she said. "Canada's refusal to address the significance of environmental protection astonishes me because climate change is an urgent problem affecting children's immediate and long-term future." The girls were inspired by then 12 year-old Severn Cullis-Suzuki's stirring speech at the 1992 Earth Summit in Rio de Janeiro. Severn became famous as "the girl who silenced the world for six minutes." At the time, Canada was a leader on global environmental issues. Oh, how the mighty have fallen; at the 2012 Climate Summit in Doha, Qatar, Canada had plummeted to 58th place out of 61 countries judged on climate change policies. We beat out only Kazakhstan, Iran, and Saudi Arabia. The influential Conference Board of Canada branded Canada an environmental laggard in a January 2013 report. According to *How Canada Performs* we rank 15th out of 17 developed nations on environmental performance, ahead of only the United States and perennial bottom dweller Australia.

THE NORTH KOREA OF ENVIRONMENTAL LAW

Canada is badly lagging the rest of the world in the race to clean, green energy. We are one of the only countries in the world to have refused to join the International Renewable Energy Agency (IRENA), which has a goal of 100 per cent renewable energy worldwide. The IRENA club includes the EU, China, the U.S., most of Africa, India, Japan, and Australia. They seem to understand the significance of the $244 billion invested in clean energy worldwide in 2012. Our snubbing of IRENA is all the more mysterious considering Canada would appear to have already attained the IRENA goal. Research by the David Suzuki Foundation shows that "Canada has more than enough solar, wind hydroelectric and biomass energy potential to meet our current and future needs for fuel and electricity."

In March 2013, the government pulled Canada out of the United Nations Convention to Combat Desertification, which fights the effects of drought around the world, especially Africa. As with Kyoto, Canada is the only country on earth to pull out of the Convention, which Ottawa ratified in 1995 and costs just $300,000 a year. Foreign Affairs Minister John Baird derisively labeled the Convention a "talkfest." Former Ambassador to the UN Robert Fowler called our withdrawal from the treaty "a departure from global citizenship. (The government) has taken climate change denial, the abandonment of collective efforts to manage global crises and disregard the pain and suffering of the peoples of sub-Saharan Africa (among many others) to quite a different level," Fowler said. Green Party leader Elizabeth May went on the hyperbole attack, saying the withdrawal made Canada the "North Korea of environmental law. The Prime Minister told this House [of Commons] that Canada legally withdrew from the treaty to combat drought and desertification because it was "...not an effective way to [use] taxpayers' money", May told the House of Commons. "The cost of the treaty, $300,000 a year, is roughly equivalent to half the cost of a G8 gazebo or 109 days of the care and feeding of a rented panda, less than 4% of the PMO office budget, a third the cost of shipping an armoured vehicle to India, or two days of government advertising to tell us how happy we should all be with the way the government is spending our money."

BIG BEVERAGE?

I [Trevor] recall being flabbergasted when bottled water products came out on the market. It seemed ludicrous that companies would bottle and charge for what came free from the tap. I duly resolved to have no truck with bottled water and predicted the quick demise of it. I of course have given in many times over the years but I learned to love them in Afghanistan where water was as essential a piece of kit as dry socks and ammunition. Beverage colossus Nestle is bottling and selling the equivalent of seven Olympic-sized swimming pools of pure BC groundwater every year for profit. The world's largest seller of bottled water drains up to 265 million litres of water from an aquifer about 150 kilometres west of Vancouver. The town of Hope also relies on that aquifer for its water. Nestle is ruthlessly taking advantage of the fact that BC is the only jurisdiction in Canada that does not charge companies for groundwater use. Draining water from a developed country with probably the largest fresh water resources in the world is irresponsi-

Trevor Greene and Mike Velemirovich

ble at best. But sucking dry a poor, developing country where hundreds of thousands of children die every year from illnesses caused by dirty water is reprehensible. Nestle is draining scarce water from the small Pakistan village of Bhati Dilwan to make its premium "Pure Life" brand, forcing villagers to drink foul-smelling sludge. A 2012 documentary, "Bottled Life," tells the whole sordid story. A village councilor tells the filmmakers that the filthy water is making the village children sick. Nestlé refused to cooperate, on the pretext that it was "the wrong film at the wrong time." One wonders if Nestle thinks the time will ever be right to expose their cruel corporate greed. It's said that every day more children die from drinking dirty water than AIDS, war, traffic accidents and malaria put together.

Trevor Greene and Mike Velemirovich

THE STORY OF FUEL

POWERED BY MOONSHINE

In the 1600s, ethanol or alcohol fuel was used for lighting, cooking and drinking. Following the American Revolution, George Washington instituted an unpopular whiskey tax to help pay for the war which ignited the Whiskey Rebellion in 1791. By the mid-1800s the first internal combustion engines were being made to run on ethanol. In 1896 Henry Ford developed his first car, the Quadricycle to run on pure ethanol. Even his renowned Model-T was designed 20 years later to run on ethanol, gasoline or a combination of both. Henry Ford was a strong proponent of ethanol along with other influential people like Alexander Graham Bell. In 1906 Teddy Roosevelt passed the Free Alcohol bill that removed the alcohol tax, which made ethanol far cheaper than gasoline. After the 21st Amendment repealed prohibition in 1933, lobbying efforts led by the petroleum industry shot down ethanol subsidies claiming they created a bootlegger atmosphere at fuel stations and they hurt the oil and auto industries. This effectively ended any prospect of ethanol becoming a viable substitute to gasoline. It would be many years before ethanol was even considered to power cars.

LIGHTING THE WAY BY WHALE

Humans have burned fats and oils from animals and plants for heat and light for many centuries. Whale oil was the fuel of choice for lighting in the

1700s. It was used for products such as soaps, cosmetics, candles, mechanical lubricants and crayons up to the late 1800s. Whaling activity around the world diminished stocks of the magnificent beasts to dangerously low numbers. It took many decades for us to better understand species extinction but it would be a century before a global moratorium on whaling [which countries like Japan and Norway are openly flouting] was established in the mid 1980s.

NUTS FOR BIODIESEL

In 1897, German engineer Rudolph Diesel invented an engine that became the workhorse of transportation around the world for over a century. His original engine was designed to run on fuel made from peanut oil — the first biodiesel. During World War II, fuel rations around the world restricted who was permitted to buy gasoline and how much they could use. In the U.S., non-essential civilian drivers were heavily restricted but essential services such as wartime workers, police officers and doctors, received unlimited fuel. Drivers throughout Europe turned to biofuel to power their cars. Tens of thousands of people used wood-burning gasification units awkwardly mounted to the nose of their car. Fuel stations throughout Europe began selling wood in place of gasoline. The next big shakeup of world fuel availability was the Arab Oil Embargo of 1973, which caused severe fuel shortages and massive line-ups at gas stations. Enterprising drivers began making their own biodiesel from used cooking oil for use in small diesel trucks and buses covered in colourful flowers. But hippies were not the only people burning homemade fuel. Farmers often powered their tractors using homemade biodiesel.

Trevor Greene and Mike Velemirovich

THE BIO-BUG

In 2003, I [Mike] bought my first 200-litre drum of pure soybean-based biodiesel to begin field tests with a brand-new diesel Beetle. Three thousand trouble-free kilometres later we had achieved the same performance as fossil fuel. In 2005, Volkswagen authorized warranty coverage for new vehicles burning biodiesel.

Even as late as 2003, diesel cars and trucks puffed out huge clouds of black smoke and particulates, but a 2007 fuel standard known as clean diesel dramatically reduced smog emission. Clean diesel eliminates the sulfur that gave old-fashioned diesel exhaust its unique smell and added a yellow hue to smog-filled skies. Clean diesel was adopted in Canada in 2012 and will be fully in place in the United States by 2014. The fuel specifications require sulfur content to be reduced by a whopping 97 per cent. The exhaust systems in clean diesel cars are so efficient that on smog alert days in large cities, the exhaust emitted from the tail pipe is cleaner than the air entering the front of the car. Modern clean diesel cars are performing like mobile air filters: a quantum leap forward from Rudolph's old peanut-burning diesel engines of 1897.

THE MYTH OF JED CLAMPETT AND THE OPEC FIX

During John F. Kennedy's presidency in the early 60s, a new socio-economic development was spreading throughout the western world. It was based on the story of a man named Jed Clampett. A poor mountaineer who barely kept his family fed. And then one day he was shooting at some food, when up through the ground came a bubbling crude. Oil that is. Black gold. Texas tea. The Beverly Hillbillies was a popular and long-running television show that perpetuated the American dream of instant wealth associated with oil. The world's first oilrig gushed in Titusville, Pennsylvania in 1859 and began an oil boom that heated homes, powered cars and improved living conditions for millions of people. By the 1970s we used so much oil that it began to run out and we became dependent on imports from OPEC nations (Organization of Petroleum Exporting Countries). OPEC began in 1960 with the best of intentions to protect small member nations from powerful and manipulative oil corporations, but OPEC itself became bloated with power and began manipulating global oil pricing. In 1973 the Arab Oil embargo brought the western world to its petroleum knees with fuel shortages and skyrocketing prices and for the first time in history we became aware of much oil we use and how little is left. Big Oil learned from OPEC and perfected the manipulation of fuel pricing at the consumer level.

When I [Mike] sold diesel vehicles, I regularly received customer complaints about diesel fuel pricing. Customers correctly pointed out that diesel fuel requires less refining than gasoline, so should cost less at the pump. Oil companies usually respond with; "Diesel fuel is essentially the same as furnace oil which is in higher demand in winter, so up go the prices". Now let me get this straight: oil companies make billions in profit and spend millions to influence politicians, but can't afford a meteorologist to predict cold weather in winter? Even Jed Clampett's nephew, Jethro, could do that. Most business people go straight to jail for price-fixing, but not Big Oil. They get a pass. To add insult to larceny, they also get billions in subsidies. In other words, consumers hand over billions of our tax dollars, so Big Oil can hold us hostage at the pump. While alternative fuels and electric cars receive a fraction of the subsidies paid to Big Oil, well-funded lobbyists lurch out of their limousines to whine about socialized industry and accuse anyone concerned about climate change of being a warmist conspirator. The tragedy in this tale is the silence of consumers whose spirits have been broken by decades of pouring subsidies into oil corporations who fix prices

Trevor Greene and Mike Velemirovich

with impunity. The delusion of instant oil wealth is a myth based on a 50-year old black and white television show. Our pressing reality is the need for a national energy policy and balanced subsidies, so we can get on with the business of developing a sustainable economy.

DIESELGATE

Amidst the glitz and glam of the 2008 Los Angeles Auto Show the sober theme was the clean automotive future promised by electrification. Volkswagen's Jetta diesel was voted the green car of the year. Jurors for the coveted award included Jay Leno, a self-diagnosed car addict, Jacques Cousteau's son, Jean-Michel and editors at the Green Car Journal. Respect for German engineering had been reaffirmed and rightly so, since strict new tier 2 emissions regulations were then coming into full effect and many people assumed that meant the death of diesel. Undaunted, Volkswagen went on the attack and invested millions of advertising dollars to buff its shiny new green halo. By 2015, VW had sold over 11 million diesels worldwide, which helped them supplant Toyota as the largest automaker on the planet. But on September 18th 2015, VW suffered a head-on collision with the US Environmental Protection Agency. The EPA issued a notice of violation of the federal Clean Air Act to Volkswagen and Audi for using software that circumvents EPA emissions standards. Volkswagen was busted. Rather than solve the Tier 2 regulations, they defeated them—Volkswagen cheated. The company faces US federal fines of up to $37,500 per car and with sales of almost 500,000 units, fines in the US alone could total $18 billion. VW will then face criminal charges and class action lawsuits by owners who feel duped and who will suffer extraordinary depreciation of the value of their cars. In the days that followed the EPA charges, VW lost a staggering $28 billion in share value, which was almost 40% of the company's value. CEO

Martin Winterkorn, who has an infamous eye for detail, resigned, saying blithely, "I am not aware of any wrongdoing on my part." Winterkorn went on to say he was, "endlessly sorry," as he walked out the door with a severance package and pension worth $67 million. Long-time fans of VW were stunned by the company's brazen disregard for the law, for the environment and for its loyal customers. How could the auto company that introduced the quirky and iconic Beetle betray its fans and its heritage so blatantly?

GM AND TOYOTA FIRST TO CHEAT

Cynics asked what all the fuss was over VW when General Motors and Toyota had been recently convicted of similar ethical breaches in which people died. That is a fair question, but on reflection, the difference is significant. The cases with GM and Toyota involved accidents caused by unintended mechanical defects that were not immediately clear. For 10 years, GM failed to recall millions of cars with ignition switch flaws that could shut down the vehicles' electrical system in mid-travel. Once the ignitions were determined to be the cause, however, GM failed to act quickly enough to recall affected models. Toyota's case was similar, although the cause was unintended acceleration. Toyota also failed to act quickly enough to recall affected vehicles. In both cases, employees and executives avoided criminal prosecution, but the companies each paid over a billion dollars in fines and legal settlements, which barely affected their bottom line. After seemingly embarrassing public hand wringing for their unethical breaches, both companies enjoyed higher sales as though nothing ever happened. So why the big stink over the VW debacle now known as Dieselgate? In a word: intent. Legally speaking, intent is everything. It's the difference between being injured in a fall and being pushed to the ground. An October 2015 study by scientists at MIT and Harvard concluded the excess nitrogen oxide resulting from VW's software defeat device would have sickened thousands of people with respiratory and cardiac conditions and probably contributed to about 60 premature deaths. Lawyers say VW could be charged with any of a number of crimes, including wire fraud (for selling cars that did not remotely justify the claims in its many advertisements) and making false statements to government officials. VW retained Kirkland & Ellis, the same lawyers who defended BP after the Deepwater Horizon disaster.

On December 10 2015, VW released the results of its internal investigation, which claimed the software malfunction was due in part to, "the misconduct and shortcomings of individual employees". Nobody on the management board was implicated in the report.

Estimates of Volkswagen's fines and lawsuits range from just a few billion to a staggering $87 billion, which would likely kill the company. Regardless of the outcome, the people inside Volkswagen who are least responsible for the situation are paying the highest price—namely the independently owned dealerships and the thousands of salespeople who cannot afford the loss of income that has resulted. I [Mike] spent 30 years working in a Volkswagen dealership and always said, "I'm not in the car business, I'm in the Volkswagen business". Volkswagen is a different kind of car company; their brand is quirky and fun and uniquely positioned to revolutionize the automotive industry like no other, except maybe the revolutionary electric car company Tesla Motors.

Rather than punish the company, redemption is the better path according to 45 green business leaders and environmental groups who wrote an open letter to Mary Nichols, chairwoman of the influential California Air Resources Board. The letter suggests Volkswagen be released from its obligation to fix the diesel cars already on the road in exchange for a full commitment to greatly accelerate the introduction of zero-emission vehicles, which would result in a, "ten to one or greater reduction in pollutant emissions as compared to the pollution associated with the diesel fleet cheating." Included on the list of signatories is Elon Musk, the founder of the most revolutionary car company in the world, Tesla.

As someone who knows and loves both Volkswagen and Tesla, I suggest Elon Musk take the idea one step further: sell Tesla to Volkswagen to combine their engineering and distribution muscle with Tesla's ground-breaking innovation that would accelerate the introduction of zero-emission vehicles tenfold.

FOOD OR FUEL

There is a raging controversy that demand for biofuel is competing with demand for agricultural crops in what is known as the "Food or Fuel" debate. Over eight million litres of gasoline, diesel and jet fuel is burned every day and there is simply not enough arable land on Earth to grow enough feedstock for that amount of fuel. The future of biofuel lays in next-generation fuels. First-generation biofuel is made from sugar, starch and vegetable oil derived from food crops. The second generation is derived from non-food crops like waste material and non-edible plant material. Third-generation biofuel holds tremendous promise, since it is made from algae that grows quickly, yields more oil per acre and can be grown in places where nothing else can survive. In order for fast-growing algae to thrive, it must be fed large amounts of carbon dioxide and this is where the real excitement begins. Research is being done to find a method to feed industrial carbon dioxide directly to large-scale algae farms in what amounts to an almost closed loop of fuel and pollution.

OIL IN A FLASH

Oil takes over 300 million years to produce in the natural world. Solazyme, a San Francisco-based firm in the advanced biofuel industry, takes just a few days. Even better, Solazyme's oil is a drastic improvement on the primordial-school product because it burns with lower emissions. In June 2011, Solazyme made history by providing the fuel for the first-ever military aircraft to fly on algae jet fuel. In February 2013, Solazyme began replacing palm, coconut and other plant oils with algae oil. Palm oil is used in a huge range of products ranging from soap to plastics. It's also a major driver of the destruction of native forests in Indonesia because palm oil farmers clear the land for their crops. Also in February 2013, Solazyme signed a $20 million multiyear agreement with Japanese trading giant Mitsui to jointly develop high-value tailored algae oils for use in household and personal care products as well as aviation lubricants. Solazyme appears to be poised to dominate the advanced biofuel industry for some time to come.

LIVING BUILDINGS

Some German builders are bringing their buildings to life using algae. At an apartment complex in Hamburg, transparent panels containing vast microalgae colonies were installed on the southern walls of the Bio Intelligent Quotient House. The algae, gathered from the nearby River Elbe, is nourished by liquid nutrients, natural sunlight and carbon dioxide. In turn, it provides dynamic shading, thermal insulation and noise reduction as well as generating power. The microalgae also consume carbon dioxide, reducing the building's greenhouse emissions. The developers say this renders the building completely carbon neutral.

GRANDFATHER TREES

The Archangel Ancient Tree Archive was co-founded in 2008 by David Milarch, a third-generation nurseryman with over 40 years of experience. Diana Beresford-Kroeger, a prolific multi-disciplinary scientist, advises Milarch. She lyrically explains the importance of the project on the group's website. "All memory is trapped in DNA, the older the better ... long ago, the master plan of DNA was tied into a carbon currency. Carbon became the living key for planetary trading. Out of a toxic atmosphere of carbon dioxide, carbon was sequestered into life forms and oxygen spilled into the atmosphere. [Ancient trees] bank the most carbon, they store the greatest carbon in reserve ," she says. "They are drought-resistant and maintain fresh water aquifers. They all, to a tree, pump oxygen into the atmosphere to maintain all life on this planet." The group collects DNA from so-called champion trees, "the last remaining representatives of our old-growth forests," clones them and plants them in Archival Living Libraries, where they can be studied for generations. In December 2012, 250 clones were planted in Oregon. The clones came from fifty 2,000 year-old redwoods now living along the California and Oregon Pacific coast, including cuttings from the 33-foot wide Fieldbrook Stump, one of the largest redwoods that ever lived. Grandfather trees are a mystical but tangible link to our past, dating back to the time of Jesus Christ. A component of oxygen has the same magical allure. About one per cent of the air we breathe is an inert gas called argon. Inert gases aren't absorbed and mathematicians hypothesise that every breath we take contains millions of argon atoms that were once breathed by ancients like Plato and Jesus.

TAR SANDS 101

Eons ago, northern Alberta was a massive lakebed. As algae and plankton

Trevor Greene and Mike Velemirovich

sunk into the sandy bottom, the heat and pressure of millions of generations of the stuff were transformed into bitumen which saturated the sandstone, creating oil sands. A company that would become Syncor first developed the Alberta oil sands in 1967. Syncrude came next and would go on to dig the world's biggest mine. Oil sands extraction is a hugely inefficient process that consumes five barrels of water for one barrel of bitumen and takes up to 1,000 cubic feet of natural gas to produce a barrel of crude. The Alberta oil reserves are the second largest in the world after Saudi Arabia. They sit under almost 150,000 square kilometres of boreal forest—an area larger than the state of Florida, and double the size of New Brunswick. This blasted heath, the biggest industrial operation on earth, can be seen from space. Such a brutal enterprise, with millions of dollars at stake, is bound to engender corruption and deceit. A 10-year veteran of the oilpatch talked about environmental infractions committed regularly at a site where he worked. He spoke on condition of anonymity because if his name was published, "I know I would be terminated and blacklisted forever in the oil patch. That is how they do things." He described a procedure called a pipe blowdown, which vents the pressure from a pipe system. The rusty red steam is heavily laden with toxic, corrosive liquid and is supposed to be stored in a lined tailings pond. Instead, the steam is "vented into the environment staining the nearby trees and buildings dark red," he says. And when the tailings ponds become too high "large-volume pumps are hooked up and the drainage water is pumped directly into the forest." This same company has the gall to trumpet a policy of Zero Harm to the People, Zero Harm to the Environment. "Should we trust the company that is going to build the pipeline up north?" he asks rhetorically about Northern Gateway. "Absolutely not. They will close sensitive areas like pump stations and areas with leaks or damaged pipes to anyone attempting to see or report problems. Once the pipeline is built the entire length of it will be posted as *No Trespassing*." A survey found that less than one per cent of environmental violations in the oil sands are subject to any prosecution. In late July 2013, a tar sands oil leak at an extraction operation in northern Alberta came to light a full nine weeks after it began. An anonymous government scientist blew the whistle after visiting the Canadian Natural Resources operation. He had pictures and documents that showed that dozens of animals, including loons and beavers, had been killed, and an estimated 60,000 pounds of contaminated vegetation had been removed.

A GENTLER WAY

Bitumen is being ripped out of the tar sands by a hellish process called the steam-assisted gravity drainage (SAGD) method, which consumes such obscene amounts of natural gas and water that the industry is desperate for a gentler method. Engineer John Nenniger may have it. Nenniger, CEO of oil sands driller N-Solv, has patented a process called Bitumen Extraction Solvent Technology (BEST) that is 600 to 800 per cent more energy efficient than SAGD. It's much cheaper too because it doesn't need water treatment or steam generators. Nenniger's technique uses propane as a solvent instead of steam. The vaporised gas warms up the bitumen to 40° C as it condenses, chewing away at the greasy stuff pore by pore. The process consumes no groundwater nor burns valuable natural gas. Nenniger, who earned a doctorate from MIT, asserts that, "from a scientific point of view this technology is a great opportunity to significantly reduce the energy requirements for tar sands extraction." In January 2015, the pilot project near Fort McMurray, which began producing in the first quarter of 2014, produced 25,000 barrels of oil.

Trevor Greene and Mike Velemirovich

A CRUEL PARADOX

A cruel but inescapable paradox of modern civilization is that the enormous expense of developing renewable energy is wholly dependent on high fossil fuel prices. And because petroleum is critically important to the Canadian economy, oil sands mining is necessary for decades to come while we build the green economy. That doesn't stop some academics from lashing out at the industry. Thomas Homer-Dixon is a professor in the University of Waterloo's Balsillie School of International Affairs and the co-author of *Carbon Shift: How Peak Oil and the Climate Crisis Will Change Canada.* He wrote an editorial in the April 7th 2013 New York Times called "The Tar Sands Disaster." In his strongly worded piece, Homer-Dixon said Canada's reliance on the oil sands "is relentlessly twisting our society into something we don't like." He also suggested President Obama would be doing Canadians a favour by blocking the controversial Keystone XL pipeline.

THE OIL GLUT MYTH & THE DOUBLE DISCOUNT TALL TALE

Oil producers have long been whining about an "oil glut" at the hub of refineries in Cushing, Oklahoma, where crude oil from the mid-continent is mixed to the specific grades required by different refineries. They claim the glut is costing the economy millions of dollars and can be solved by laying more pipeline. Economist Robyn Allan mightily begs to differ. She says the dreaded oil glut has been carefully planned by Big Oil since 2006 to access new markets and should naturally unblock by 2014 as technical difficulties with refinery and pipeline capacity expansion are solved, all without a kilometre of new pipeline being laid.

Oil sands crude, such as Western Canadian Select [WCS], is always going to be more expensive as compared to the North American benchmark

West Texas Intermediate (WTI) because it takes more energy to upgrade it before it can be refined into commercial products. This is a natural, permanent discount that no amount of pipelines can solve. The "double discount" is allegedly caused because there is a discounted price for WTI as compared with the international benchmark Brent and then the second discount comes when the Alberta crude is released to the market. Allan has a problem with this one too: "the double discount is a hard luck con. It creates public sympathy for multinational pipeline companies such as Enbridge, Kinder Morgan, and TransCanada who want to build pipelines, and multinational oil producers such as Suncor, Total, Imperial Oil and national oil companies owned by foreign governments, like the Chinese National Offshore Oil Company, who want to export raw resources."

Allan says the con pushes a bitumen export strategy not in Canada's interests. "The con is designed to allow the world's wealthiest industry to achieve supernormal profits by granting them an unfettered public license to build 'all pipelines, going anywhere' for an unrefined resource." Allan gave a searing indictment of Canada's energy strategy in April 2013. She said that the policy of exporting raw oil sands bitumen "is determined in the boardrooms of a handful of multinational corporations and by the governments of foreign countries through their state-owned oil companies. The strategy is communicated to the federal and provincial governments through closed-door meetings with lobbyists and at state dinners over dessert in foreign countries."

HOT AIR IN QATAR

The world has been gathering to discuss the imperiled environment since 1988 in Toronto when politicians and scientists concluded that "humanity is conducting an unintended, uncontrolled, globally pervasive experiment whose ultimate consequences could be second only to a global nuclear war." Over the next 26 years, what Time Magazine called "the annual exercise in futility that is the U.N. climate summit" has been staged around the world and has consistently produced daily dramatic walkouts, finger-pointing, stall tactics and peacock-like posturing. Almost 200 nations met in Doha, Qatar in late November 2012 in yet another high-profile attempt to hammer out a U.N. deal to curb global emissions of greenhouse gases by 2020. Opinions were mixed about the wisdom of having an OPEC member like Qatar host a summit on fossil fuels and there was a furious controversy over the choice of summit president. Not only was Abdullah bin Hamad al-Attiyah Qatar's oil minister and a former president of OPEC, but he had been named the best petroleum executive in the world in 2007. These concerns appear to have been borne out by the fact that interventions from non-governmental organisations groups during the talks were limited to a farcical 30 seconds. Wael Hmaidan, director of the Climate Action Network International, said that tensions were high but "if Qatar puts an [emissions reduction] pledge forward it could transform the whole mood and help Qatar do its job as President."

THEATRE OF THE ABSURD

Al-Attiyah presented the 2012 Best Petroleum Executive in the World Award to none other than "a very distinguished executive" Fu Chengyu, the Chairman of the Board of Directors of Chinese petro behemoth SINOPEC, "in recognition of his outstanding contributions in the oil and petroleum industry." Ten days later, Al-Attiyah opened the Doha Climate Summit. The Economist's headline that week was *Theatre of the Absurd* and charted the complex failures of previous Summits. "… at Durban [2011], with the obligations that Kyoto put on rich countries about to expire, countries promised more talks about talks, saying they would negotiate a new climate regime by 2015 and have one in force by 2020. The Doha meeting began that negotiation."

Canada's Environment Minister Peter Kent gave an interview to the Globe and Mail before Doha. Kent stated that Canada would not soften its hard line on Kyoto or sacrifice economic growth to cut emissions. One of UN climate chief Christiana Figueres' three priorities for the Doha Summit was commitment of financial aid for poorer countries to fight climate change. Kent flatly rejected this measure, saying our federal government wouldn't put up new money for the fund. Kent asserted that the summit is "not a pledging conference." His combative stance earned Canada a satirical "fossil award" from environmentalists at the summit. It marked the sixth year running that Canada has taken the dubious honour. Prominent UK journalist George Monbiot called Prime Minister Harper "an irresolute wimp" for his failure to keep Canada's promise to cut emissions by six per cent. Canada fell woefully short of 2012 emissions targets and in December 2011 became the first country to pull out of Kyoto, the world's only binding climate treaty. Environment Minister Peter Kent told the House of Commons two hours after returning from the Durban climate talks that the government had "no choice given the economic situation." Canada is home to the most mining companies in the world so our fossil fuel lobby no doubt exerted its massive influence to manipulate the pullout.

SITTING IN A ROOM SIGNING A PIECE OF PAPER

The reaction from around the world to Canada's rejection of Kyoto was swift and unsparing: Xinhua, the official news agency of China, called the withdrawal "preposterous" and "irresponsible." The UN's Christiana Figuerosa diplomatically said the decision was "regrettable" and "surprising." Anne Applebaum is a Pulitzer Prize-winning author, prolific journalist and academic. Applebaum wrote in the July 2009 issue of Slate magazine before the disappointment of the Copenhagen Climate Summit: "the truth is that carbon emissions will not be reduced by international bureaucrats, however well-meaning, sitting in a room and signing a piece of paper." When all the posturing, drama and backroom scheming was done on December 8 2012 the Qatar Summit closed — as the pundits said it would — with an extension to Kyoto but few legitimate emissions agreements. For the first time, the rich nations officially and, it is to be hoped, permanently, agreed that they should compensate developing countries for losses due to climate change.

MORE HEAT THAN LIGHT

The poor nations, of course, hailed that almost-pledge as a major breakthrough, but condemned the massive gulf between the harsh truths of the science and the political will that will have to be brought to bear to tackle climate change. The eulogy for the latest round of ponderously slow talks about talks about the urgent need to act quickly was written by Irish Times columnist Frank McDonald whose column on December 10, 2012 ran under

the headline *Doha Climate Conference Yields More Heat Than Light:* "...
the UN Framework Convention on Climate Change process is governed by
consensus and characterised by compromise, so what often emerges is the
lowest common denominator; an agreement to move forward with which
almost no one is entirely happy, but that is widely recognised as the best
available at the time."

The Warsaw Summit lived down to expectations, managing to gasp out only
a vague draft text on the last day about when countries should present their
targets for restricting carbon emissions, a key element of the deal that's supposed to be adopted in Paris in 2015. On November 13th, the second day of
the summit, the Canadian government officially abandoned any pretence of
support for global action on climate change by congratulating Australia for
scrapping its two-year old carbon tax in late November. Stephen Harper's
press secretary droned, "...the Australian prime minister's decision will be
noticed around the world and sends an important message."

REDEMPTION AT LAST

The City of Lights has been the setting for historic peacemaking over the
years, beginning with the Paris Peace Conference of 1919 that ended the
First World War. In 1973, the Vietnam War was officially ended in Paris and
in 1991, the carnage between Cambodia and Vietnam was laid to rest in Paris. For two weeks in early December 2015, the eyes of the world were on the
climate talks in Paris in the hope that a planetary peace deal would be forged
to combat global warming. On Saturday December 11th, shortly after 7.25
p.m. local time, climate summit president Laurent Fabius rapped his green,
leaf-shaped gavel and made history; "Looking out to the room I see that the
reaction is positive, I see no objections. The Paris agreement is adopted."

Green Party leader Elizabeth May has been a tireless advocate for the environment all her life. There is no better person to explain the implications of the Paris Agreement;

I have been working on climate for the last 29 years. In that time I have seen lip service from most politicians, courage from a few politicians, venality from some corporations (Exxon come to mind), leadership from others. I have witnessed opportunity after opportunity squandered for political expediency. Agreements signed and then ignored. Overall we have procrastinated and lost decades when we could have averted the climate crisis nearly entirely. Now we are in it; loss of life and devastating droughts and heat waves, extreme weather events, sea level rise and loss of Arctic ice and permafrost. No longer are we arguing about a future problem. We have already changed the climate, so the debate of 2015 is "can we avoid the very worst of the climate crisis? Can we ensure the survival of human civilization? Can we save millions of species?" To do so requires transitioning off fossil fuels. You will undoubtedly hear some denounce the Paris Agreement for what it does not do. It does not respond with sufficient urgency. It does not use the levers available to governments to craft a treaty that is enforceable with trade sanctions to add some teeth. Those criticisms are fair. As trade lawyer Steven Shrybman said more than a decade ago "If governments cared as much about climate as they do about protecting intellectual property rights, we would have laws that require carbon reduction in every country on earth." Nevertheless, the Paris Agreement is an historic and potentially life-saving agreement. It does more than many of us expected when the conference opened on November 30. It will be legally binding. It sets a long-term temperature goal of no more than 1.5 degrees as far safer than the (also hard to achieve) goal of no more than 2 degrees. In doing so, it may save the lives of millions. It may lead to the survival of many small nations close to sea level. It may give our grandchildren a far more stable climate and thus a more prosperous and healthy society. It clearly means the world has accepted that most known reserves of fossil fuels must stay in the ground. It is absolutely true that Canada announcing support for 1.5 degrees mid-way through the conference made a huge difference in keeping that target in the treaty. I heard that from friends and contacts around the world. To avoid 1.5 requires immediate action. Unfortunately, the treaty is only to take effect in 2020 (after it is ratified by 55 countries, collectively representing 55% of world greenhouse gas emissions). We have built into the treaty mandatory global five-year reviews—what is called the "ratcheting up mechanism." The mechanism to force all governments to assess the adequacy of their own plans only kicks in in 2023. That gap from 2015 to 2023 could well foreclose any option to hold temperature to less than 1.5 or even 2 degrees.

In addition to the Paris Agreement we also passed the Decision of COP21 [Conference of Parties, the formal name of the Paris climate summit]. It includes some actions before 2020. The language there is far from perfect but gives us a chance to increase targets before 2020. Canadians can be rightly proud of what our government did in Paris. While I did not support our position on every single issue, I cannot be more proud of what we did on most issues, nor can I thank our newly minted Minister of Environment and Climate Change, Catherine McKenna, enough for her work.

What matters now is what we do next. Canada's climate target remains the one left behind by the previous government. We have no time to waste in re-vamping and improving our target. We should be prepared to improve it again in 2020. But let's ensure we get started. The Liberal platform committed to hold consultations with all provincial and territorial governments within 90 days of COP21 . In his speech at COP21, Trudeau expanded that to engaging with municipal governments and First Nations as well. That is

Trevor Greene and Mike Velemirovich

all excellent. Ideally this sets in motion a quick-start to identifying a more ambitious target with actions spelled out in the spring 2016 budget.

Earth Day 2016 has been chosen in the decision document as the day for formal signatures to the Paris Agreement. UN Secretary General Ban Ki-moon has been requested to organize a signing ceremony at UN headquarters in New York.

Paris threw us a lifeline. Don't let it slip between our fingers.

KEYSTONE DIPLOMACY

Because the proposed XL pipeline crosses the Canada-US border, the State Department is the responsible agency. The State Department's March 2013 review of the project stated outright that the pipeline will spill oil. Not *may*, but will. The same review estimated that it would create only 20 to 50 permanent, operational jobs in the U.S. and 2,500 to 4,650 temporary jobs. US Secretary of State John Kerry talked pipeline with Canadian Foreign Affairs Minister John Baird in February 2013. Kerry said he was "luke-warm" on the pipeline and told reporters that he is waiting for reports from a review process started by his predecessor Hillary Clinton. Kerry refused to be pinned down on a timeline for his decision and, according to Macleans magzine, hoped to make a call "in the near term. I'm not going to go into the merits of it here today."

WALKING ANOTHER LINE

Just as the filmmakers Frank Wolf and Todd McGowan did along the Northern Gateway, writer Ken Ilgunas walked from the source of the Keystone XL pipeline in Hardesty, Alberta, to its terminus in Port Arthur, Texas, five months later. "I'm doing this to understand the situation the best I can," Ilgunas told a local newspaper at the halfway mark. "You really can't understand the land and the people that might be affected until you see it or hear from them. It's one thing to be here, it's another thing to just look at a map."

The route of the 1,897 kilometres of pipe traced nearly 1,750 water bodies and cut through the Ogallala Aquifer, one of the world's largest underground sources of fresh water and the source of drinking water for millions of people. The Aquifer is over a thousand feet deep, but in many places, you can literally stick a stake in the ground and hit water. Then there's the mighty Missouri River. The Toronto Star journalist who was embedded with my [Trevor's] platoon in Afghanistan is now the Washington bureau chief and one of the best journalists I know. Mitch Potter and a colleague traced the 4,000-kilometre path of the Keystone pipeline route from Montana to Texas in 2012. Mitch spoke to Edgar Garwood, 91, who has been working his acreage on the north bank of the river in Montana for more than 60 years. His son, Ron, continues the family tradition nearby and told Mitch about the topography of the river. "Last year's rains were so great that the pressure had to be released down the dam spillway. It came straight at us with such force it changed the shoreline right where they plan to bury the pipeline," said Ron. "Then just look at the other side; the pipeline has to climb hundreds of feet up through unstable glacial hills. Where do you think the oil goes if there's an event that ruptures the pipe?" TransCanada tried to soothe their many concerns, insisting the pipeline will dip to eight metres from the standard 1.3 metres under the three main rivers along the way.

BAD TIMING FOR A BREAK

The case for XL wasn't helped by a spill of thousands of barrels of diluted bitumen from an aging Exxon pipeline in the small Arkansas town of Mayflower on April 2nd 2013. The video of oil flowing across lawns and down streets from the ruptured 65-year old Pegasus pipeline went viral shortly after being released. Exxon was fined in 2010 for infrequent inspection of that very line. Aging pipelines are apparently the norm according to a 2011

Trevor Greene and Mike Velemirovich

report by the US Department of Transportation. That report said most of the cross-country pipelines were built prior to the 1950's " ... in response to the huge demand for energy in the thriving post-World War II economy." In early December 2012, three young activists locked themselves inside a segment of the Keystone pipeline in Texas to protest construction. In the morning, they took pictures of sunlight shining through cracks in the welding seams on the top of the pipe. When they came out of the pipe, they were arrested and held in jail for 24 days. Shortly after the arrest, TransCanada discreetly laid that segment of pipeline in the ground. In 2012, there were 364 pipeline spills in the US — just short of one a day — oozing about 54,000 barrels of oil and refined products, according to the US Pipeline and Hazardous Materials Safety Administration. Toothless PHMSA regulations mandate that only seven per cent of natural gas lines and 44 per cent of hazardous liquid lines be inspected. Incredibly, Exxon won't face a fine of any kind for the Arkansas spill because of a loophole that could have been designed for the situation: the diluted bitumen that befouled the bucolic town of Mayflower is not classified as oil. The bean-counter wriggle ensures that ExxonMobil, which reported profit of $44.88 billion in 2012, will not have to pay into the federal Oil Spill Liability Trust Fund. In November, 2013, the PHMSA fined Exxon a paltry $2.6 million, 0.01 per cent of its 2012 profit of $45 billion.

MOTHER NATURE FILED HER COMMENTS

On March 1, 2013, the US State Department reported that the Keystone XL pipeline poses no threat to the environment and "approval or denial of the proposed project is unlikely to have a substantial impact on the rate of development in the oil sands, or on the amount of heavy crude oil refined in the Gulf Coast area." That prompted Bill McKibben to retort, "here we are again, with the State Department producing basically the same report they produced before, saying there will be no big impact from this pipeline… Mother Nature filed her comments last year—the hottest year in American history." Shortly after the report came out, the sheep's costume came off. It turns out the "sustainability consultancy" commissioned to write the report, Environmental Resources Management (ERM), was directly under contract to TransCanada to write the report. ERM based its report on information supplied by two oil industry contractors: EnSys Energy, which has worked with Exxon, and ICF International, which reportedly works with oil and pipeline companies. The report's release ushered in a 45-day public comment period before the final environment report will be published.

The revered science journal *Nature* said President Obama shouldn't be trying to appease environmentalists like McKibben by turning down the pipeline but instead should take on the coal-engorged power and utility companies in the US. One of the biggest objections to the pipeline is that it would be pumping "dirty" tar sands oil. The world's most-cited science journal said tar sands oil is not as dirty from a climate perspective as many believe. It said some oil produced in California is worse but flies under the environmentalists' radar. Scientific American took the opposite tack in suggesting in its June 2013 piece *Oil Sands May Irrevocably Tar the Climate* that Keystone "…will be a spigot that speeds tar sands production, pushing the planet toward its emissions limit."

BOLD PRESIDENTIAL WORDS

A New York Times editorial on March 10, 2013 sought to hold President Obama to his promises: "a president who has repeatedly identified climate change as one of humanity's most pressing dangers cannot in good conscience approve a project that — even by the State Department's most cautious calculations — can only add to the problem." It recalled Obama's hard-line stance on global warming that so gladdened environmentalists: "…in his State of the Union address, President Obama pledged, "if Congress won't act soon to protect future generations, I will." On June 25th 2013, the President showed his bold words weren't just rhetoric. Obama told students at Georgetown University that he refuses to "condemn your generation and future generations to a planet that's beyond fixing." He hinted, for the first time, that approval of the Keystone XL pipeline might not be a slam-dunk, and for climate change-related reasons. "Our national interest will be served only if this project doesn't significantly exacerbate the problem of carbon pollution," Obama said.

After President Obama stayed true to the promise he made at Georgetown and quietly put the boots to Keystone XL in early November 2015, the announcement subtly faded away in the roar of the nonstop news cycle probably because for seven interminable years the star-crossed scheme had environmentalists chaining themselves to inanimate objects, rabid right-wing types in Canada shrieking about getting 'our product' to tidewater like teenage drug dealers talking about their weed and rabid right-wing types in the US invoking the bible as justification for the pipeline and pissing and moaning about lost jobs. But said right-wingers clearly weren't privy to, or, as is much more likely, willfully ignored, a report from the State Department that said Keystone would spawn only a fraction of permanent, operational jobs in the U.S. that the Republicans claimed would be created. In 2013 President Obama called bullshit on these claims saying that after it is built, "…we're talking about somewhere between 50 and 100 jobs in an economy of 150 million working people."
But that's just a guess for the unusual tranquility surrounding Obama's

long-telegraphed cancellation of the project that prompted then-prime minister Stephen Harper to impertinently assert to the most powerful man in the world that XL was a 'no–brainer.' But the death knell sounded only for the northern cross-border portion. TransCanada quietly began construction of the southern leg of the controversial pipeline in August 2013 near Livingston, Texas. Hollywood actress Daryl Hannah was arrested alongside Eleanor Fairchild, a 78-year old great-grandmother. Hannah stood by Fairchild as bulldozers and excavators razed her 300-acre East Texas farm and its natural springs that produced more than 400 gallons of fresh water per minute. But Eleanor and Darryl would have gone ballistic had they known that there is already a Keystone pipeline carrying Alberta bitumen. Launched into service in June 2010, Keystone 1 is a narrower pipe than the controversial XL version. And it is very leaky: no fewer than 14 spills since the taps were turned on.

Most of the incidents were small, except for the spill early one bad morning in May 2011, when 20,000 gallons of tar sands exploded into the tiny town of Cogswell, North Dakota. And there may be many more Cogswells in the future because Calgary's Enbridge Pipelines [shudder] has been pumping tar sands oil from Alberta to Texas since December 2014 along a daisy chain of pipelines that are a clone of Keystone XL. Yes you read that right. The clowns who killed Michigan's Kalamazoo River are RIGHT NOW pumping hundreds of thousands of barrels of toxic tar sands bitumen the length of the US every day. A full-blown inquiry conducted after the Kalamazoo spill laid bare the full extent of Enbridge's embarrassing buffoonery. Upon hearing that it took the company 17 hours and 19 minutes—three full shifts—to turn off the gush of oil after a gas company employee notified them, Deborah Hersman, the chairperson of the inquiry into the spill said,

Trevor Greene and Mike Velemirovich

"...you can't help but think of the Keystone Kops [there's that word again]. Why didn't they recognize what was happening? What took so long?" Apparently incompetence and an almost criminal lack of giving a shit were what took so long. The inquiry found operators were confused about the warning alarms or how they were to respond. They not only failed to diagnose the breach but twice tried to restart the pipeline with alarms sounding repeatedly. Enbridge started a costly cleanup; a billion dollars and counting because five years on, the Kalamazoo is still filthy—and will be so for the foreseeable future because the Environmental Protection Agency says the river is so fouled that additional cleanup might do more harm than good.

As the debate raged and the cross-border rhetoric went nuclear over Keystone XL, the rocket scientists at Enbridge were craftily and quietly shipping hundreds of thousands of barrels per day of tar sands bitumen from Alberta. This line, cavalierly called the Alberta Clipper, which at first shipped 450,000 barrels a day from the tar sands is designed to carry an astounding 800,000 barrels a day to Illinois. From there, the bitumen crawls into the so-called 'pipeline crossroads of the world' in Cushing, Oklahoma and finally on to the terminus at Port Arthur, Texas and then to the global markets.

Trevor Greene and Mike Velemirovich

TO CRACK THE EARTH OPEN

James Glave writes a blog on Canada's transition to an economy based on clean and renewable energy and clean technology. This "tweet" is on his website: *I sure am glad our government decided to keep Canada's coal power plants running until 2056,"* said nobody, ever. Coal is everywhere. And it's cheap. And like oil, it is very energy-dense so the power it produces is very cheap. Therein lies the climate change conundrum: renewables would increase the average North American family's power bill from $100 per month to $150 or higher. Banking giant Citigroup said in an April 2013 report that it expects renewable energy to eventually come to fruition but at a high cost: it will require much more natural gas than we're currently using. There is a symbiotic relationship between fossil fuels and renewables because when the sun isn't shining or the wind blowing, backup power plants, called peaker plants have to be brought online to provide power. Peaker plants typically run on natural gas. Like all fossil fuels, natural gas has become ever harder to extract, so an extraction technique right out of a bad action flick has come into vogue: fracking.

THE CIVILIZED PATH UNTAKEN

Bill McKibben wrote an article about fracking in the May 8th 2012 New York Review of Books. "We could, as a civilization, have taken [the] dwindling supply and rising price [of oil] as a signal to convert to sun, wind, and other noncarbon forms of energy—it would have made eminent sense. Instead, we've taken it as a signal to scour the world for more hydrocarbons." McKibben quotes author Seamus McGraw's description of fracking: "having drilled a hole perhaps a mile deep, and then a horizontal branch perhaps half a mile in length, you send down a kind of subterranean pipe bomb, a small package of ball bearing-like shrapnel and light explosives. The package is detonated, and the shrapnel pierces the borehole, opening up small perforations in the pipe. Then pump up to seven million gallons of a substance known as slick water to fracture the shale and release the gas. It blasts through those perforations in the pipe into the shale at such force — more than nine thousand pounds of pressure per square inch — that it shatters the shale for a few yards on either side of the pipe, allowing the gas embedded in it to rise under its own pressure and escape." The oil and gas industry is fond of saying fracking is safe because "its been a proven technology in the field for 60 years." Cornell University engineer Anthony Ingraffea is one of the world's foremost authorities on the science of fracking. He says the claim to 60 years has just enough of a kernel of truth to allow the industry to justify the claim. The frackers are dating themselves from a crude fracking operation that was built in Kansas by a small US oil company in 1947.

FUGITIVE GAS

Every year, fracking leaks about 126 billion cubic feet of methane into the atmosphere. Methane is hugely more powerful than carbon dioxide as a global warming agent. Local people all over the northeast US near fracking sites reportedly suffer from chronic illnesses and birth defects. The industry is correct in claiming natural gas produces less carbon dioxide when it's burned compared to oil and coal. But the shale gas from fracking is more

Trevor Greene and Mike Velemirovich

energy intensive and emits high amounts of carbon dioxide and hydrogen sulfide. So-called "fugitive methane" costs natural gas producers $1.5 billion a year and is one of the most destructive aspects of fracking. It seems a quick, obvious solution to just fix the leaking pipelines but methane is colourless and can be odourless, making it hard to tell when it's escaping. Responsibility is another issue: the producer owns the gas, but an independent contractor owns the actual pipeline. Methane only makes up 10 per cent of greenhouse gas emissions but its warming power is 20 times stronger than carbon dioxide. That being said, the greenhouse property of a gas is measured over a hundred years and methane only lasts about 10 years in the atmosphere while carbon dioxide lingers much longer. And, methane makes up only nine per cent of greenhouse gases. So, by the crude calculus of climate catastrophe, carbon dioxide from burning coal is waaay nastier [pardon the scientific jargon] than methane from fracking.

KILLING FARMERS AND CATTLE

The Nation magazine profiled North Dakota cattle farmer Jacki Schilke in November 2012. Five of her cows had dropped dead since 32 fracking oil and gas wells began operating within three miles of her ranch. Schilke developed a limp and chronic pain in her lungs and had recurring rashes for a year. Schilke's doctors diagnosed her with neurotoxic damage and constricted airways. "I realized that this place is killing me and my cattle," Schilke says. The farmer stopped eating her own beef and the vegetables from her garden. A test of the farm air found "elevated levels of benzene, methane, chloroform, butane, propane, toluene and xylene — compounds associated with drilling and fracking, and also with cancers, birth defects and organ damage." Schilke's well tested high for sulfates, chromium, chloride and strontium.

Josh Fox made a documentary film on fracking called *Gasland* in 2010 after he was made an offer from a gas company for rights to find gas deposits on his Pennsylvania property. Pennsylvania, New York, Ohio, West Virginia and nearby states sit on the Marcellus Shale Formation, a massive reserve of sedimentary shale that holds an estimated $2 trillion worth of natural gas. Fox finds glasses of tap water that look like dark beer and reek of chemicals. He watches one man actually light his tap water. What Fox didn't say was that methane occurs naturally in groundwater aquifers worldwide, and people have been getting their kicks from lighting their tap water for some time. Be that as it may, a natural resource extraction method that is so grotesquely destructive that it causes serious illness and birth defects should be far more closely regulated than it is at present.

MAKING THE EARTH SHAKE

Oklahoma recorded the largest earthquake in its history in 2011. The epicentre was within a kilometre and a half of three active wastewater injection wells, which are abandoned oil boreholes used for wastewater storage after oil drilling operations. Professor Katie Keranen, an expert in geology and geophysics at the University of Oklahoma, says when pressure builds in these disposal wells, it pushes up against geological faults, sometimes causing them to rupture and set off an earthquake. Kernan lives not far from the three wells in the quake zone and measured the tremors with a seismometer. "Without question, there is a strong likelihood that [the quake] was induced," Keranen said. Scientific American says more than 30 trillion gallons of toxic liquid has been injected deep into the American ground over the past several decades. Natural gas seems to be abundant and is pitched as an inexpensive energy source for decades to come, but that is only part of the story. If we combined the cost of fracking perils with fossil fuel subsi-

Trevor Greene and Mike Velemirovich

dies, then the true price of natural gas would be much higher. There are some who say it is time to think the unthinkable to make fracking an unpleasant, distant memory.

Trevor Greene and Mike Velemirovich

PANDORA'S PROMISE

Editorializing in the UK's Independent newspaper in 2004, renowned scientist James Lovelock, shocked the mainstream environmental movement by voicing support for nuclear power: "Sir David King, the Government's chief scientist, was far-sighted to say that global warming is a more serious threat than terrorism. Nuclear energy has proved to be the safest of all energy sources," he said. "Its worldwide use as our main source of energy would pose an insignificant threat compared with the dangers of intolerable and lethal heat waves and sea levels rising to drown every coastal city of the world." Lovelock said that worrying about getting cancer from nuclear radiation is pointless taken in the context of global warming. "We must stop fretting over the minute statistical risks of cancer from chemicals or radiation. Nearly one third of us will die of cancer anyway, mainly because we breathe air laden with that all-pervasive carcinogen, oxygen." Other high-profile proponents of nuclear energy are Christine Todd Whitman, former New Jersey governor and head of the Environmental Protection Agency, respected scientist James Hansen and billionaire philanthropist Bill Gates. In 2013, Academy Award-winning director, Robert Stone, made a controversial documentary called *Pandora's Promise,* which argues in favour of nuclear energy. The film follows five leading environmental activists who had become pro-nuclear because they realized that the measures used to fight pollution haven't made a dent in climate change.

BREEDING POWER

Pandora's Promise argues that the problem with nuclear is the outdated technology, developed when the Cold War raged, of light-water reactors instead of new-generation breeder reactors. A breeder reactor can run off of the fuel it produces at a higher rate than it consumes. It basically breeds. This fuel can be cycled many times through the reactor as opposed to the light water reactors, which have only one cycle. The film makes the startling assertion that only wind turbines are safer than nuclear. It then claims that many more people are killed by air pollution from burning coal than from nuclear energy generation. Renowned earth scientist James Conca says "the poorly-considered drive to swap nuclear with natural gas and gas-dependent renewables will erase the recent benefits gained from replacing old coal plants with gas. " Even nuclear-skeptic Al Gore has started to come around to the merits of the new generation of reactors. On the seven-year anniversary of *An Inconvenient Truth* in May 2013, Gore said, "if they can successfully build these smaller, safer, passably safe modular reactors that come in smaller increments at an acceptable cost, then I think we could see a renaissance in the nuclear industry, 10, 15, 20 years from now." Westinghouse Electric will definitely be part of that renaissance. The same company that made your blender and toaster started fuel tests for its Small Modular Reactor (SMR) in 2013. The SMR produces only 225 megawatts, far smaller than traditional reactors, but can be built in pieces and assembled on-site. Its containment vessel is 89 feet tall as opposed to a traditional reactor's 250 feet. The SMR is cheap to build because it uses standard turbines from General Electric rather than custom-made parts from overseas.

Trevor Greene and Mike Velemirovich

FISSION VS FUSION

The challenge of where to store nuclear waste has long held back construction of new nuclear plants in the US. Bill Gates might have the answer. Gates has spent hundreds of millions of dollars on a Washington-based company called TerraPower, which is developing a reactor designed to run on the depleted uranium found in nuclear waste. Terrapower's traveling-wave reactor (TWR) would be fired up by enriched uranium then burn nuclear waste for decades without refueling. Gates says he became interested in the reactor's potential to produce cheap, zero-carbon energy and its ability to turn "what is a waste product into fuel." TWRs would require far less fuel and maintenance than today's reactors. John Gilleland, TerraPower's CEO, thinks they could have a prototype by the early 2020s. Terrapower uses fission, or conventional nuclear energy technology, which splits atoms to create energy. Fission's controversial cousin, fusion, generates energy by joining atoms together. A theory called "net gain" is the holy grail of nuclear fusion: an almost endless supply of clean electricity with virtually no radioactive waste. A small British Columbia company has developed an unorthodox fusion process that is competing with the fusion heavyweights.

HUNTING THE GRAIL FROM A GARAGE

The theory that sound waves could be used to trigger a fusion reaction dates back to the 1970s at the U.S. Naval Research Laboratory in Washington D.C. A world and decades away from those sparkling, well-equipped labs and sparkling, well-educated scientists, a motley BC company called General Fusion is well into the hunt for the net gain grail. The General Fusion reactor is a metal sphere that looks like a truck engine with bulbous arms sticking out on all sides. Inside the sphere, a shock wave is forced through a mixture of chemicals. The theory goes that the force is so great it will cause the mixture to compress and merge into helium, which would cause a fusion burst, setting off temperatures that only occur at the core of the sun. It is a bold, innovative method that hasn't been tried before. In September 2001, General Fusion's president and chief tech officer Dr Michel Laberge quit his job designing cutting-edge lasers in Vancouver. Then he actually lived the cliché of garage startup, beavering away in a rented garage on Bowen Island, a West Coast hippie enclave. Four years later, Laberge came up with his game-changing idea to revolutionalise nuclear fusion. CEO Doug Richardson said General Fusion hopes to accomplish a controlled reaction by 2016 at a cost of about $40 million. Funding will come from Federal grants with the rest coming from private investors like Amazon.com founder Jeff Bezos.

From his garage, Laberge realized the fast microprocessors, advanced materials and space-age control systems that he had used to make his lasers could make a mechanical fusion reactor actually work. An early private investor was venture capitalist Michael Brown who told the Toronto Star in 2013 that he has faith that General Fusion has figured out cold fusion. "I keep looking for people who will say to me that this isn't going to work, and I can't find that person," says Brown. "It's not just that they're going to prove net gain first. If they prove it, they're light years ahead of everybody else in terms of being able to make electricity." In the academic arena, the General Fusion concept is either cheered or jeered. One unabashed fan is esteemed Berkeley plasma physics professor Dr. T. Kenneth Fowler. Fowler told Canadian Business that he found out about General Fusion when he attended a talk given by Laberge in 2007 at the University of California. "This may be the best idea I've heard. It probably resonated with me because I published a paper that wasn't all that different. (General Fusion) just went for a shorter time scale." One of Canada's leading particle physicists, Erich

Vogt, leads the jeer section. Vogt, who helped found TRIUMF, Canada's national laboratory of nuclear and particle physics in Vancouver, refers to General Fusion's lab as "Cloud Cuckooland" and calls their theories "unproven science in the guise of technology development."

THE GHOSTS OF NUCLEAR PAST

The spectres of Three Mile Island, Chernobyl and Fukushima hang over the nuclear dilemma like ... well ... radioactive fallout. But, according to the World Nuclear Association, the accident at Three Mile Island in Pennsylvania wasn't a cataclysmic event. At 4 a.m. on March 28th 1979, a malfunction in the cooling system caused a reactor to partially melt down. The final report notes that, "some radioactive gas was released a couple of days after the accident, but not enough to cause any dose above background levels to local residents." Not a single case of cancer has been attributed to the incident. Chernobyl is synonymous with nuclear catastrophe. A routine test of operations in case of power loss was being carried out on April 26th 1986 at 1:23 a.m. at the Chernobyl nuclear energy plant. Extreme power spikes caused several explosions in reactor number four. The resulting fire sparked a Cold War nightmare: a massive cloud of radioactive fallout drifted into the atmosphere. The evil cloud loomed over large parts of the Soviet Union and Western Europe and there were dire predictions of thousands of deaths. But a 2005 study of the disaster by the International Atomic Energy Agency and the World Health Organisation found that in the 20 years since the disaster at Chernobyl fewer than 50 people have died as a result of the incident. An inquiry determined that the engineers who designed the test were specialists in electric generators, not in nuclear reactors and inexplicably there was scant consultation with actual nuclear reactor engineers during the procedure preparation.

The disaster at Fukushima was a catastrophe of biblical proportions that surely can only happen once a millennia. In general, nuclear is carbon free and modern technology makes it about as safe as airplanes—accidents are very bad but very rare.

Trevor Greene and Mike Velemirovich

BANGKOK SINKING, AUSTRALIA BURNING

Coal is the filthiest of the fossil fuels, accounting for over 40 per cent of US carbon dioxide emissions and the largest source of mercury pollution. We [Trevor] Cape Bretoners have a saying about the filthy rich that "they can pay God to make the sun rise in the west and set in the east." Australia is the world's top exporter of coal, mostly to Asia, and there are two filthy rich and controversial Aussies who dominate the coal industry. Nathan Tinkler first saw the inside of a coalmine as an apprentice electrician. He was 30 years old in 2006 when he sold his home and electrical-contracting business to raise the $1 million to buy an undeveloped coalfield close to two mining operations. By 2008, his mine was worth $530 million. Tinkler is a hefty lad whose attitude and grace hasn't kept pace with his net worth. In 2010, Tinkler responded to a reporter's questions somewhat abruptly, "you're a fucking deadbeat, people like me don't bother with fucking you. You climb out of your bed every morning for your pathetic hundred grand a year, good luck." Tinkler bought a pro rugby team and a stable of racehorses. In 2012, he bought a luxury home on Singapore's Millionaire Row near the other Aussie mining magnate. Some believe multi-billionaire heiress Gina Rinehart will be the world's richest person by 2014 as her coal and iron projects mature and earn her annual profits of as much as $10 billion. There must be something in the DNA of Aussie miners that make them court controversy. Rinehart's public pronouncements have made her the subject of such headlines as *12 Reasons Why So Many People Hate Australian Billionaire Gina Rinehart*. Rinehart's comments about "jealous" poor people and her call for a wage cut for Australian miners didn't win her any friends. Rinehart, daughter of a virulent racist, is a climate change denier and is embroiled in a nasty, public lawsuit with three of her four children over control of the trust fund started by their grandfather. In March 2012, they reached an agreement to extend Rinehart's control of the trust until 2068. By then, Rinehart would be 114 years old and the youngest of her three children would be 83.

THE DESTRUCTION OF THE BIGGEST LIVING THING ON EARTH

The endangered Great Barrier Reef, the world's largest living structure, has the misfortune to lie along the coast of mineral-rich Queensland. And not even a designation by UNESCO as a World Heritage Site is likely to be a lifesaver. In July 2013, the Australian government proposed building new coal terminals at the deepwater port of Abbot Point. There are nine proposed "mega mines" nearby that at full capacity would release 705 million tonnes of CO_2 into the atmosphere annually, according to Greenpeace Australia. The United Kingdom by comparison, emitted a total of 550 million tonnes in 2011. Three million cubic metres of material would have to be dredged from the ocean floor to allow access for large cargo ships. Reef scientist Terry Hughes told the Australian Senate that "… based on the science, large amounts of dredging will simply hasten the ongoing decline of the Great Barrier Reef." Scientists say that since 1986, the reef has lost half its living coral, and could lose 95 per cent of its coral by 2050 should ocean temperatures increase by the forecast 1.5 degrees Celsius. Residents and business groups in the area are enthusiastic about the economic windfall the project will bring.

Trevor Greene and Mike Velemirovich

Environmental groups are also challenging the port expansion in court amid concerns the dredging and dumping will damage the nearby Great Barrier Reef, potentially causing further delays to the expansion, which is expected to take more than two years. India's Adani Group has warned it may scrap plans to expand its coal terminal at Queensland's Abbot Point if dredging of the sea bed cannot be completed next year, because it could incur $1 billion in losses annually from export delays.

Billionaire businessman Gautam Adani has personally asked Prime Minister Malcolm Turnbull to introduce a law that prohibits activist groups from seeking judicial review of environmental approvals for major projects such as Adani's proposed $15 billion coal mine, rail and port project in Queensland.

Sandeep Mehta, chief executive of Adani Australia Coal Terminal, has told Queensland's Minister of Environment there is "a real risk the project will not proceed" if dredging does not occur between March 1 and June 30, according to legal documents filed with Brisbane's Administrative Appeals Tribunal that have been obtained by Fairfax Media. "Adani will also suffer at least one year's worth of losses associated with not having cargo moving through the export port," Mr Mehta said in an affidavit.

Adani's losses if the port expansion does not proceed by 2017 are expected to run to about $1 billion annually because it will not be able to export thermal coal from its $16 billion Carmichael mine.

AUSTRALIA BURNING

A new colour had to be added to the temperature map of Australia on January 7th 2013 to mark temperatures of 54 degrees Celsius in Eucla, Western Australia. Nationwide, Australia had its hottest day on record that day with an average of 40.33 Celsius. Four of Australia's hottest 10 days on record have been in 2013. Yet, there are still many Australians who don't see what all the fuss is all about. Prominent UK journalist George Monbiot wrote in the January 8th Guardian that "climate change denial is almost a national pastime in Australia." Opposition leader Tony Abbott has perfected the art of doubting the science and impacts of climate change, insisting constantly that "the science is highly contentious, to say the least." Abbott has long resisted attempts by Prime Minister Julia Guillard to curb runaway emissions that have made her country the world's leading per capita emitter of carbon. Monbiot says the *Australian* newspaper "takes such extreme anti-science positions that it sometimes makes the [UK tabloid] Sunday Telegraph look like the voice of reason." Abbott once dismissed the science of climate change as "crap." Abbott took aim soon after Guillard introduced the divisive, unpopular carbon tax on July 1st 2012. Abbott immediately vowed to abolish the tax if elected. Shortly after winning a landslide victory in September 2013, Abbott set about keeping his promise; introducing repeal legislation the very first day he entered Parliament as PM.

WHERE DO WE PUT BANGKOK?

In 2011, Thai lawmakers studied the world's first-ever proposal to consider moving a national capital city. Anond Snidvongs, a climate change expert at Bangkok's Chulalongkorn University bluntly says if no action is taken to protect the city, "in 50 years … most of Bangkok will be below sea level." Bangkok, which is known as the Venice of the East for its canals, is slowly sinking, as is the real Venice. Being only two metres above sea level and built on swampland makes life hard on Bangkok's 12 million citizens. The Chao Praya River runs right through Bangkok and floods the mega-city every summer in the monsoon season.

There are 20 million Bangladeshis in cities like Barguna, Chittagong and

Cox's Bazaar who are no doubt twitchily eyeballing the tides. These coastal cities will be the first to be inundated when the sea level rises by a metre or more by 2100 if climatologists are right. Bangladesh is constantly hammered by storm surges that wreak havoc up to 100 kilometres inland. A diplomatic furor in the Bay of Bengal has been oddly resolved by sea level rise. Both countries claimed a flat, muddy patch of land west of Calcutta. What the Bangladeshis called South Tolpatti and the Indians knew as New Moore Island has sunk beneath the waves forever.

MYSTERY SOLVED?

In September 2012, New Zealand refused refugee status to a man from the island nation of Kiribati who said on his application that he fears for his children's future on Kiribati, which is elevated just slightly above sea level. Kiribati is 32 coral atolls astride the equator over 1,350,000 square miles of ocean. I [Trevor] began my military career in the regular force navy. The biggest adventure of my short stint in the Navy was sailing the Pacific from Victoria to Australia on the navy sail-training tall ship HMCS Oriole. Crossing the equator in 1997, we made port at Kanton Island in the Kiribati chain and I likely sailed past the island of Nikumaroro. The Kiribati chain has distinctively smooth flat coral reefs on which a small plane could conceivably be crash-landed. There is compelling evidence that famed aviator, Amelia Earhart and navigator, Fred Noonan, survived a crash landing in the Kiribati chain during their 1937 attempt to fly around the world at the equator. Nikumaroro is some 350 miles southeast of Howland Island, their destination. Analysis of Earhart's last radio transmission indicates that her aircraft was likely on land and on its wheels for several days following the disappearance. A British Colonial Service officer on Nikumaroro in 1940 found the human remains of an individual "more likely female than male, more likely white than Polynesian or other Pacific Islander, most likely between 5 feet 5 inches and 5 feet 9 inches in height." There were campfire sites nearby and signs that seabirds and shellfish had been eaten and rainwater collected. A woman's shoe, a jar of freckle cream (Earhart was very self-conscious about her freckles) and a sextant box whose serial numbers are consistent with a type known to have been carried by Noonan were also found. In May 2013, the International Group for Historic Aircraft Recovery took a sonar image in the reef off Nikumaroro that could be a wing or part of the fuselage from Earhart's aircraft. The object is estimated to be at least 34 feet long and arrow-straight, which indicates a man-made object. It was the tenth expedition of the tenacious US government-funded group to the island. Nikumaroro is overrun by nocturnal coconut crabs the size of small dogs. My [slightly grisly] theory is that the two adventurers — if it was Earhart and Noonan — survived the crash, made their way to shore and, at least for a few weeks, trapped birds, gathered shellfish and collected water to survive. Gradually, Earhart and Noonan became so weakened by exposure to the elements and lack of food that one night they were unable to fight off the voracious, swarming crabs.

THE SLOW DEATH OF THE MALDIVES

The star of The Island President is rotting in jail. Mohamed Nasheed, the charismatic former president of the Maldives, was sentenced to 13 years in prison in March 2015 for ordering the arrest of a senior judge in 2012. The capital, Male, exploded in violence in response. Thousands of Nasheed supporters clashed with police ever since Nasheed's arrest in February. The trial was pretty much the textbook definition of a travesty of justice; Nasheed was repeatedly denied access to lawyers, denied the right to appeal, and his defence witnesses were prevented from taking the stand. His arrest

Trevor Greene and Mike Velemirovich

of Judge Abdulla Mohamed in 2012 led to weeks of unrest and forced Na-sheed to step down as the Maldives' first democratically elected president. Nasheed's win ended the 30-year rule of dictator Maumoon Abdul Gayoom. Nasheed, who was known as "the Mandela of the Maldives," was arrested and tortured many times under Gayoom's regime. After a coup by forces loyal to Gayoom, Nasheed resigned on February 7, 2012. Current president Abdulla Yameen Gayoom is the half-brother of former dictator Maumoon Abdul Gayoom. Apparently, relatives of Maldivian dictators can just take over the reins of power when convenient. The latest unrest comes amid concern about increasing Islamist militancy in the country and growing opposition to Yameen's rule. His conviction effectively prohibits Nasheed from running in elections in 2018. Nasheed issued a call to arms to his supporters: "To change this government and work towards forming a government that would pave the way for the people's development and prosperity; to not be afraid of being arrested or facing a long sentence; to take all of your lives in your hands and to go out onto the streets in protest." The Maldives is a collection of atolls that adorn the Indian Ocean north of the equator like teardrops. With most of the Maldives' 1,200 islands nosing only one metre out of the Pacific south of India, about 360,000 Maldivians live with the constant danger of being forced to evacuate their homeland. Its highest point of land soars two and a half metres above the beach. The nation is in danger of being reduced to a network of interesting new reefs by 2112. Nasheed starred in the documentary _The Island President_ about his efforts to lobby world leaders to proactively fight against climate change. He held the world's first underwater cabinet meeting in October 2009 to draw attention to the plight of the Maldives. Wetsuits replaced pinstripes and hand signals and waterproof white boards were used to draw up a document calling on all countries to cut their emissions. The soggy communiqué read, "we must unite in a world war effort to halt further temperature rises. Climate change is happening and it threatens the rights and security of everyone on Earth." The Maldivians set a good example. The entire country is committed to carbon neutrality by 2020, every child is educated in environmental science and they have furiously built retaining walls around every island. In November 2008, Nasheed announced plans to buy land in India, Sri Lanka, and Australia for his people if the danger of inundation becomes too great. He famously told British parliamentarians that being carbon-neutral " ... is not going to stop us from annihilation. But at least we can die knowing that we've done the right thing." It's surreal and oddly disconcerting to think of political corruption, vote-rigging and torture afflicting an island paradise like the Maldives when the place is so indelibly associated with a noble, desperate battle against global warming. We almost wish the vagaries of political intrigue were limited to cold, hard Northern Hemisphere countries so we can get on with our cheerleading for the plucky Maldivians as they desperately fight to stay afloat.

THE FIRST CLIMATE REFUGEES

The Inuit village of Shishmaref, Alaska has been settled for 4,000 years and rivals the Maldives for the most dramatic example of rising seas in the world. Situated on a tiny island on the edge of the Arctic Circle, Shishmaref is literally being swallowed by the sea. An elder estimates the tide moves an average of three metres closer to the land every year. The whole village is due to relocate to the mainland — which means the people of Shishmaref, a community in the developed world, will probably claim the dubious distinction of being the first climate refugees in the world.

A manmade environmental disaster is being perpetuated in Brazil that could make climate refugees out of the Stone Age tribes of the Amazon.

Trevor Greene and Mike Velemirovich

THE LUNGS OF THE EARTH

The Chilean poet, Pablo Neruda, lyrically described the Amazon rainforests as the lungs of the earth. Brazil appears poised to collapse those lungs on a paradoxical quest for a solution to global warming. The 1.4 billion-acre Amazon Basin, which makes up half the world's tropical forests, is estimated to hold 10 billion tonnes of carbon. Brazil is looking primarily to hydroelectric energy as its major power source but also as their clean green solution to combat global climate change. About 151 dams are planned for the Amazon. However, their plan to build "at any cost" the third-largest dam in the world is being fought tooth and nail on the home front and internationally. Nine billion hectares of rainforest will be forever altered. The host of critics of the colossal Belo Monte dam have made the project synonymous with abuse of indigenous tribal rights. When the builders accidentally dynamited a sacred burial site, the indigenous Arara tribe took action, taking 100 workers hostage, demanding that construction stop and the company pay $5.7 million compensation for the loss of the burial ground and pollution damage to the river. They had caught almost no fish in the preceding two years, forcing them to rely on farmed fish provided by the government. Experts estimate that huge clouds of methane would bubble to the surface from the rotting trees of the flooded rainforests. The dirt-poor farmers who will be flooded out aren't placated with the government's promise of temporary work. They see no value in the trade-off for their land and the river fish they have lived on for centuries. The Belo Monte dam is planned for the Xingu River, an Amazon tributary that crookedly ambles north for 1,230 miles from the mouth of the Amazon. More than 25,000 indigenous people from 40 ethnic groups depend on the resources of the Xingu. Construction began quietly in March 2011, the start of Carnival in Rio, probably not coincidentally, when most Brazilian eyes were firmly fixed on the spectacle of the country's annual carnival. By 2015, there was a thin brown line across the mighty Amazon with pristine river water above and trails of ugly, oily sludge downriver. Right now, verdant green rainforest is being transformed overnight by growling yellow construction equipment into pale brown switchback roads that lead to colossal craters. Five thousand men work in two shifts, from early morning until 2:30 a.m., six days a week. The dam is half complete and is only the first in a planned network of mega-dam projects. Brazil's drive to develop the Amazon is ostensibility a clean green solution for energy security and wealth but can they put a price on the Amazon and the indigenous peoples who also rely on the Xingu River for their security? Only time will tell what the true cost of Belo Monte will be.

THE SAUDI ARABIA OF LITHIUM

Bolivia has an Amazon development row of its own. For much of 2012, it tried to build a 182-mile highway, 32 miles of which would cut through a vital ecosystem located at the geographic heart of South America that links the Andes range and the Amazon basin. But environmental studies show that the highway will contaminate three main rivers and open huge tracts of jungle to illegal logging and settlement. The project would also irreversibly alter the habitats of endangered species and rare primates, which would threaten the traditional way of life of three endangered indigenous cultures. The highway project is a component of a Brazilian-led initiative,

Trevor Greene and Mike Velemirovich

The Initiative for the Regional Integration of South America (TIPNIS) — an ambitious scheme that calls for 531 massive infrastructure projects in and among the bruised ecosystems of the Amazon basin. The TIPNIS road project has, unsurprisingly, created an uproar. Indigenous groups have marched on the capital and clashed with police, which has created a thorny political challenge for Bolivian President Evo Morales, who is the country's first indigenous leader. In 2010, Morales made history when the United Nations accepted his proposal to make water a human right. In an open letter in 2008, Morales wrote, "in the hands of capitalism everything becomes a commodity: the water, the soil, the ancestral cultures and life itself. Humankind is capable of saving the earth if we recover the principles of solidarity, complementarity and harmony with nature." Morales has been lauded around the world for his opposition to developed countries' addiction to oil and consumerism. He has always called for consultation with indigenous people before development projects are given the go-ahead. Therein lies the rub. Morales leads South America's poorest nation. But a full 13 per cent of Colombia's GDP comes from mining. The revenue from Morales' 2006 nationalization of the hydrocarbon sector has been well spent on social programs like education and childcare. Morales must walk the fine line between crusading for Mother Earth and caring for poor Bolivians. Morales is drawing that line in salt.

In 1976, the world's largest deposit of lithium was discovered in Bolivia underneath the world's highest salt lake. The Uyuni Salt Flat covers 3,900 square miles of flat desert plateau in Bolivia's Andes Mountains. Some suggest that their vast reserves of the emerald-coloured liquid — half the world's supply — can make Bolivia the "Saudi Arabia of lithium." Lithium is expected to become a crucial compound in this century and beyond because it is lightweight and can store more energy than almost any other alternative. This makes it ideal for rechargeable batteries used in hybrid and electric cars. Morales has pledged that Bolivians will sustainably exploit the lithium reserves on their own and for the benefit of Bolivians. He has repeatedly said, "Bolivia wants partners, not masters." He knows his history and is loathe to repeat the devastating cycle of raw material extraction that enriches the developed countries that take the precious material and leaves the indigenous people poor and pissed off.

PLAINTIFF MOTHER NATURE

In September 2008, Ecuador became the first country in the world to encode the rights of nature in its Constitution. The law dictates that nature in all its life forms has the right to "exist, persist, maintain and regenerate its vital cycles" and people have the legal authority to enforce these rights on natures' behalf. The ecosystem itself can be named as the defendant under article 71. The first case under the new article was won on March 30th 2011. The court of Loja province, on the southern border with Peru, granted an injunction in favour of nature, specifically the Vilcabamba River, against the provincial government of Loja. The judge ruled against a proposal to widen the Vilcabamba-Quinara road, which would have dumped tons of rock into the Vilcabamba River. The project had been in operation for three years without studies on its environmental impact.

In November 2012, Ecuador tried to auction off a huge swath of pristine Amazonian rainforest — Ecuador's last remaining tract of virgin rainforest — but encountered fierce protests at home and around the world. The Rainforest Action Network claims that between 2000 and 2010 there were 539 oil spills in Ecuador. The seven indigenous groups who live on the land are furious that they haven't been consulted on the auction. Ecuador actually has a secretary of hydrocarbons and Andres Donoso Fabara sneered,

Trevor Greene and Mike Velemirovich

"these guys [indigenous people] with a political agenda, they are not think-ing about development or about fighting against poverty." He reminded ev-eryone in March 2013 that "we are entitled by law, if we wanted, to go in by force and do some activities even if they are against them."

The lure of oil wealth in Ecuador has divided two sisters who were insep-arable as kids in the remote community of Sana Isla on Ecuador's Napo River. Two generations ago, the Kishwa tribe of Sana Isla were still using blowpipes and had only recently made contact with the outside world. The tiny community is in one of the most biodiverse places on Earth. Scientists say a single hectare in this part of the Amazon contains a wider variety of life than all of North America. The country's biggest oil company, Petroam-azonas, has made an offer to start seismic surveys in their homeland. Blanca Tapuy and her sister Innes are at loggerheads over the offer, with Blanca saying she is willing to die to stop its advances and Innes passionately as-serting that petrodollars are vital for the future of the community, which numbers only 422 residents on 43,000 hectares. Many have to paddle along the Napo river or hike through the jungle to attend community meetings on the divisive, heartbreaking issue. In January 2013, Petroamazonas finally backed down. The devastating trials and heartbreak of the sisters and their tiny home are being repeated across the Amazon but petrodollars aren't al-ways the cause. There is a new breed of predators loose in the green jungles of the Amazon. They are scam artists called carbon cowboys.

RIDE OF THE CARBON COWBOYS

Perhaps the most infamous carbon cowboy of them all is an Australian named David Nilsson. Australia's *60 Minutes* did a hidden-camera segment on Nilsson in July 2012. Nilsson, who flogged nonexistent five-acre lots in Queensland in the 1990s, boasts in the segment of having rights to three million hectares of forest in Peru under a 200-year contract. The deal with naive, poor, illiterate tribes basically gives Nilsson full rights to do anything he wants to the trees. On camera, Nilsson lays out his ruinous scam: "... my contracts are 200-year contracts, etched in stone, so when the carbon's gone, people can come through and harvest the rainforest there. We'd have a forest management plan they can reforest, they can plant palm oil, and they can cut all the timber. No one can stop them. No one can stop them." Nilsson has been carbon scamming for years, from Papua New Guinea to the Philippines. According to the Sydney Morning Herald, Nilsson sees himself as being in the forefront of a South American industry that will supply heavy-polluting businesses in Australia and other developed countries with the overseas carbon offsets they will need to meet their greenhouse gas cuts back home. Incredibly, Nilsson sees himself as a benefactor to his victims, telling the Herald, ''this could be some kind of anthropology project — tribal people in the modern world. I'll get a good model set up and really pump the training into them. Not just pump it into them, but put them under contract and loan them the money to go to university." The natives Nilsson is referring to are the Matses tribe who still hunt with bows and arrows in the virgin forests, six days by boat from Iquitos, the largest city in the Peruvian rainforest. Not exactly typical candidates for university. The Matses are the traditional owners of more than 400,000 square kilometres of pristine jungle. Nilsson's contracts are written in only in English and not in Spanish because "the World Bank and the [United Nations] only recognise the English language and the law of England and Wales for carbon projects."

ORTEGA'S ENVIRONMENTAL CRIME

When the French tried to build a canal through Panama in 1880, malaria, yellow fever and other tropical nastiness wiped out 20,000 people and the project went bankrupt. It was a project of superlatives; the largest-ever earthen dam, the most massive canal locks ever envisioned and the largest gates ever swung. At the same time, the United States was looking at Nicaragua as a more feasible location than Panama to connect the Atlantic and Pacific but gave up on the idea when they bought the Panama Canal in 1902. The concept of a Nicaraguan canal was given new life in 2013 when a Chinese company was granted a 50-year lease to dig a monstrous canal to rival the Panama Canal. The Nicaragua Interoceanic Grand Canal, as it is known, has a neat price tag of $50 billion— a billion for every year of construction. The canal project was rammed through in three days and done "in total secrecy," according to critics.

Legislators complained that congressional committees had only two days to review a bill that will irrevocably re-shape the destiny of the country and almost surely destroy an environmental treasure. Ortega's Sandanista government has grown increasingly authoritarian and secretive since he slid into power in 2007 with a narrow victory over a divided opposition. In December 2013, Ortega steam-rollered a constitutional amendment that removed presidential term limits and strengthened the role of the military in government. The bill gives Hong Kong-based HKND Group a 50-year concession to build a canal linking the Atlantic and Pacific. Nicaragua would be paid a paltry $10 million a year. HKND was founded three years ago by an enigmatic billionaire named Wang Jing owns a telecom company, Xinwei Telecom Technology, that has strong connections to the military; twice a day Wang plays People's Liberation songs in the company's Beijing headquarters. Speculation is rife that China's government is a backer of the project. Political analysts say the canal would achieve Beijing's goals of broadening China's footprint in Latin America and deflating the economic importance of Hong Kong as the primary entry point to China. Nicaraguan opposition lawmakers are predictably furious, saying preferential treatment for foreign investors in such a momentous project amounts to a violation of nation sovereignty. If built, the new canal will likely be more than 250 kilometres long, three times longer than the Panama Canal and be much wider to allow passage by the next-generation 15,000-container ships. But, construction to widen the Panama Canal to handle these massive ships is expected to be finished in 2015, and the widened canal to re-open in early 2016—three years before Nicaragua's canal is scheduled to be open, seemingly making it redundant. In a tragic irony, Nicaragua currently gets half of its electricity from renewables and that figure is predicted to rise to 80 per cent in a few years. Unfortunately, all that green energy won't be nearly enough to offset the canal project's gargantuan carbon footprint. It will probably bisect ecologically sensitive Lake Nicaragua, which is nick-named mar dulce, or "sweet sea." The lake is Central America's largest and the source of drinking water for hundreds of thousands. Canal construction would destroy around 400,000 hectares of rainforests and wetlands. Jaime Incer is the silverback of conservation efforts in Nicaragua. "There are alternatives for linking one ocean to the other, but there are no alternatives for cleaning a lake after a disaster has happened," he told Nicaragua's Confidencial newspaper. "We don't have another Lake Nicaragua." A Chinese business analyst said that Wang's project is "absurd" in its lack of environmental feasibility. Indigenous groups also say they have not been adequately consulted. They have called on the country's Supreme Court to repeal the law allowing the construction of the canal. Protests quickly grew violent. On Christmas Eve 2014, about 50 peasants were injured and a policeman was shot in a protest in the village of Rivas, where construction has begun. Police and soldiers are joining Joint Chinese-Nicaraguan teams in assessing properties along the canal's route. "There is intimidation towards the owners of the houses. They

Trevor Greene and Mike Velemirovich

feel as if they were terrorists," one municipal official said. The narrative of the canal project closely tracks that of Canada's controversial Northern Gateway pipeline, especially warnings from critics that the plan is being rushed through "...without adequate scrutiny of the environmental impact, business viability and public wellbeing."

Of course, the employment/economic benefit drum is being beaten by the government; "This will be the largest project in Latin America in 100 years," project executive Ronald Maclean boasted in 2013. Wang has promised that half of the 50,000 jobs per year during the five-year construction period will go to Nicaraguans, with 25 per cent to Chinese workers and 25 per cent from other countries. However, the Nicaraguan workforce is mostly illiterate and untrained and would be unqualified for any but the lowest-paid labourer jobs. "In the first place, it's not a Nicaragua canal, it's a Chinese canal," said a prominent Nicaraguan economist. "The biggest Chinese banks are going to finance it and the biggest Chinese businesses will build itotherwise there won't be a canal." Others are resigned to the realities of decision-making in a one-party state. "You know the Comandante — he's the boss," a shopowner said, referring to Ortega. "If he says it's going to go, it's going to happen."

Former Sandanista guerilla leader Ortega toppled hated dictator Anastasio Somoza 30 years ago and implemented liberal policies on literacy, gender equality and health care. He looks on the canal as the second phase of the Sandanista revolution. By ramming through this ruinous canal, Ortega has come full circle to reinvent the brutal regime he destroyed and is committing a heinous crime against the environment. Like the Belo Monte dam on the Amazon, the trade-off between a pristine natural treasure and the potential wealth from the proposed canal is a Faustian bargain that will only enrich the elite and destroy the way of life of millions of the disenfranchised underclass.

Trevor Greene and Mike Velemirovich

BIG SOLAR

As of April 2013, Texas had more solar workers than ranchers, and California had more of them than actors. For the U.S. as a whole, solar energy production accounts for up to 119,000 jobs, more than the number of coal miners. On May 23rd 2013, California set a new record for solar generation, then proceeded to break it the next day.

Goal Zero is a Utah-based startup that makes portable solar power charging systems and is another of those cool companies we all want to work at. The website bills itself as "a business created by people who live life to its fullest, with a shared vision inspired by the passion for adventure, respect for the planet and a humanitarian heart." They make solar chargers for cell phones and laptops but can go large to solar charging systems for TVs and fridges. Their products are not reserved for tiny boutique operations run by gear nerds but are available through mainstream US retailers.

Solar power is a funky, hip way to generate energy. Crowd-sourcing is a funky, hip way to raise capital. In January 2013, they were combined with spectacular results. A company called Mosaic instituted a program that allowed people to earn interest from small investments in solar energy projects in the US. The company's co-founder, Billy Parish, told the New York Times he thought it would take a month to raise the money. The projects were sold out in a day. Mosaic had spent just $1,000 on marketing. In 2012, super-investor Warren Buffett — who is not known for backing lightweights — invested in a California solar operator called Topaz Solar Farm. The New York Times reported, "It was the first time a public bond offering for a U.S. photovoltaic power project had been deemed investment grade."

FLIGHT OF THE SUN BIRD

An airplane powered solely by the sun flew from San Francisco to Phoenix on May 4th 2013. It was the first leg of a flight across the US that made stops in Dallas and St. Louis on its way to Washington D.C. and New York City. The Solar Impulse is a Swiss invention that was launched in 2003 and made the world's first solar flight in 2010. The carbon fibre plane weighs as much as a small car, has the wingspan of an airbus and puts out the power of a motor scooter. Solar energy is gathered from 12,000 solar cells built into the wings, which recharge four large batteries that permit night flight. The plane's solar cells are the thickness of a human hair. The Solar Impulse can reach 28,000 feet and screams along at an average of 69 kilometres per hour. Two private investors from Switzerland, Bertrand Piccard and Andre Borschberg built the plane and flew it across the US. Piccard, who made the first ever non-stop balloon flight around the world, has an impressive pedigree: 80 years ago his grandfather, Auguste Picard, pioneered high-altitude ballooning and was the first man to see the curve of the Earth. In 1960, his father, Jacques, piloted the bathyscaphe Trieste seven miles down to the bottom of the Marianas Trench, the world record for the deepest-ever dive. He took Auguste along for the ride, making him a man of both extremes; flying the highest and diving the deepest. Piccard the younger explains that pioneering is "not only what you do. It's how you think. It's a state of mind more than action."

There was some drama on the final leg to New York City on July 7th; an eight-foot tear in the fabric was spotted on the lower side of the left wing. The glitch forced the cancellation of a triumphant final photo op: the Solar Impulse soaring by the Statue of Liberty. "The goal is not to arrive as soon as possible because what is interesting with Solar Impulse is not the speed, it's the duration," Picard said. "You can theoretically stay airborne forever

Trevor Greene and Mike Velemirovich

because during the day the sun is enough to power the electrical engines and to load the batteries so it can continue to fly at night." The Washington Post artfully put the journey of the Sun Bird in perspective: " ... the Solar Impulse's journey, in many ways, is a microcosm of our nation's love/hate relationship with renewable energy. We love the promise of clean energy and celebrate the arrival of the latest green gizmos, but we have very little patience for renewable energy strategies that take years, if not decades, to pay off." The two adventurers plan to journey around the world in 2015.

THE VOYAGE OF THE SUN BOAT
Another example of Swiss solar power technology made a historic journey in 2013 across another frontier, the vast Atlantic. The Turanor PlanetSolar is a 31-metre catamaran that took only 22 days to make the 2,867-mile crossing from the Canary Islands off Spain to Saint Martin in the Caribbean. The ship looks futuristic, with solar panels covering the deck and two wings. The Atlantic crossing was just a hop for the mighty PlanetSolar. On September 27th 2010, she set off west from Monaco to circumnavigate the globe; 585 days, 28 countries, three oceans and 11 seas later, the PlanetSolar was back in Monaco, making port in May 2012.

MOJAVE STEAM
There is a massive solar plant being built in California's Mojave Desert that has no solar panels. Instead, Ivanpah has 300,000 computer-controlled mirrors that reflect sunlight onto vats of water on top of three giant towers. The water is heated to 500 degrees and powers a steam turbine. The mirror fields are massive — the Ivanpah facility is 3,500 acres — and look like bright alien crop circles in the desert arrayed around three airport control towers.

The technology of using focused sunlight to turn a steam generator is called concentrated solar power and has been around for about 20 years. The $2.2 billion project is one of the monstrous solar power projects being installed by California to meet its goal of getting 33% of its power from renewable sources by 2020. Ivanpah delivered its first flow of power to the grid in September 2013. When it goes fully online at the end of 2014, Ivanpah will provide enough energy for 140,000 homes.

SOLAR JUSTICE

A New York-based company called MPOWERD Inc. is bringing what it calls solar justice to the 1.6 billion people who are energy poor, combined with the 1.5 billion others who are either off the grid or can't afford it. Six social entrepreneurs founded MPOWERD as a benefit corporation, a new class of for-profit companies that maximize social impact, not profits. CEO Jacques-Philippe Piverger says, "within the renewable energy space we saw an opportunity for innovation to have greater impact on the lives of the disenfranchised. We call our tool solar justice, and we intend to participate significantly in the quest to eradicate energy poverty through products like Luci."

Luci is a game-changer. It's a solar-powered light that is compact, durable, user-friendly, and, critically, affordable. Luci means light in Italian. It's plastic, packs flat and inflates to the size of a coffee can. Luci could be the magic bullet that sets the energy-poor people of the world free of their dependence on unhealthy kerosene and wood fires. The founding philosophy is "... to empower the developing world through solar power, providing greater equity to those without access to electricity."

After charging for four to eight hours in the sun, the lantern provides six to 12 hours of diffused light. Senior Director of Business Development and co-founder John Salzinger describes Luci as a "bright, safe and green light that can be used by anyone living off-grid." He says Luci is having a big impact in the southern hemisphere especially. "Children can complete their nighttime homework, entire families don't have to huddle around one candle or dangerous kerosene lamp, and girls and women can walk through a slum or to the latrine without being as afraid of being attacked as they otherwise would be." Salzinger points to one study that shows the incident of rape and violent crime goes down 20 to 50 percent when light is introduced.

Plato paid tribute to the "torch bearers of humanity: its poets, seers, and saints, who lead and lift the race out of darkness, toward the light. They are the law-givers, the light-bringers, way-showers, and truth-tellers, and without them humanity would lose its way in the dark." The good people who conceived Luci are lighting the way forward for billions of the energy-poor choking on kerosene fumes and smoke.

HOW THE PLAYING FIELD GOT UNEVEN

In 2010, subsidies for global renewable energy businesses totaled $66 billion. In 2012, subsidies to the fossil fuel industry neared the $1 trillion mark. Most of these subsidies have been encoded for a hundred years, enacted to lend traction to the then-nascent oil industry. Over time, they became more elaborate and entrenched. Renewable energy companies began receiving federal subsidies in 1980 under President Ronald Reagan, but, since they are not an "integrated" or "embedded" part of the tax code, alternatives must renew their subsidy requests every year.

ON THE WIND

Like solar, wind power is plentiful, renewable, widely distributed and does not emit greenhouse gases during operation. These advantages make it one of the best renewable energy options and wind farms are being built all over the world. But eventually turbine blades wear out and have to be replaced and as more wind turbines are built, more used, football-field-sized turbine blades are being thrown out. Over 34,000 blades in the U.S. need to be replaced every year and approximately five times that many around the world. Some American researchers received a grant in September 2012 to manufacture blades using new sustainable, bio-derived materials. Conventional blades are made of fiberglass and very hard to recycle. The researchers are working on creating blades from vegetable oil derivatives. If they build an eco-friendly blade successfully, this technology will be applicable to any product that is made from fibreglass. In 2012, the U.S. had enough wind power to meet the electricity needs of more than 14 million homes. More wind-generating capacity was added than any other electricity-generating technology. Surprisingly, the home of big oil, Texas, led the way in overall wind development. Only four *countries* outside the U.S. have more installed wind capacity than the state of Texas.

Trevor Greene and Mike Velemirovich

THE DAWN OF THE HORSELESS CARRIAGE

John Rockefeller could, at a stretch, be considered the instigator of the global warming crisis. His Standard Oil aggressively cornered the US oil market in the late 1800s when alcohol was the fuel of choice by carmakers like Henry Ford. Rockefeller funded and aggressively lobbied for the prohibition of alcohol in 1919 that wiped out rural alcohol producers; potential rivals to his gas stations. Prohibition ushered in the age of the automobile, which had a precarious, peculiar start that engendered outrage, vehement opposition and bizarre controversy.

WHO KILLED THE HORSELESS CARRIAGE?

For thousands of years, horses were the primary source of transportation as they carried people and their loads, pulled carts, plowed fields and fought wars. The muscle of either man or beast did work of any kind. Horses thrive on only grass and water and conveniently reproduce themselves, so prior to the early 1700s it was difficult to imagine a better way to get around. A giant stride toward the Industrial Revolution was taken in 1712 when English inventor Thomas Newcomen invented the steam engine to remove water from mines. As steam technology improved, the first self-propelled steam carriage was invented in 1784 and a new form of personal mobility was born: the horseless carriage. Throughout the 1700s and 1800s, horse bus services, similar to the stagecoaches of the American west, were popular throughout the United Kingdom. But their hooves dug into the unpaved roads and the narrow wheels of the coaches scored deep ruts in the soft dirt. As steam technology progressed in the railway industry and in land transport, horseless carriages became popular in England and France, because they could maintain faster speeds, and wouldn't run away with customers as horses occasionally did. More important, they were much cheaper to operate than horses, could climb steeper hills and carry much larger loads. Despite its many benefits, the horseless carriage was regarded as a threat both by horse bus companies and by the emerging railway industry, so in the mid-1800s an emotionally charged lobbying campaign against the horseless carriage raged. As Queen Victoria ruled England and Charles Dickens published *Great Expectations,* the British government passed the Locomotive Act of 1861 that restricted the weight of horseless carriages and limited speeds to just ten miles per hour: far slower than a horse. To accelerate the death of the horseless carriage, Parliament passed the Locomotive Act of 1865, also known as the Red Flag Act, that further reduced speeds to just six miles per hour and required that horseless carriages be preceded by a man waving a red flag.

Change can be stressful and even frightening to some people and even new technology that clearly improves lives often meets resistance. This is when engineering must become communication — selling — in order for the new technology to be understood and adopted. Biased special interests often interfere with the communication and adoption of new technology. Abraham Lincoln abolished slavery in America against special interest groups that warned of economic ruin. Almost simultaneously that same disingenuous economic warning successfully killed the world's first horseless carriage.

Trevor Greene and Mike Velemirovich

THE MOTHER OF THE AUTOMOBILE

While the British were trying to kill their car business with red flags and intrusive laws, German engineer Nikolaus Otto was inventing the world's first four-stroke, internal combustion engine, which won him the grand prize at the 1867 Paris World Exhibition. Rudolf Diesel, a German engineer, built the first diesel engine in 1897. Early versions of Diesel's engine ran on peanut oil, but petroleum became the fuel of choice, as it was more plentiful and cheaper. In 1886 Karl Benz patented his "motorwagen." A brilliant engineer who epitomized German craftsmanship, Benz did not simply retrofit a carriage with a motor; he designed and built all the major components. By 1888, the *Benz Motorwagen* was a three-wheeled vehicle with a gas engine that generated three quarters of one horsepower with a speed of just thirteen kilometres per hour. Popular opinion of the day said the noisy contraptions were just a fad and not a practical means of daily travel. People knew horses had served them well for thousands of years, so were ambivalent about attempts to improve on that popular mode of transportation. Karl Benz was plagued by self-doubt and began to question the future of the horseless carriage. Benz's strong-willed wife, Bertha, had no doubts about her husband's brilliance or about the huge potential of motorized vehicles. Benz grew up poor, so did not have the means to save his financially struggling engineering firm. Bertha, however, came from a wealthy family and in 1871 was able to convince her father to invest her dowry into Benz's company to allow him to pursue his dream. She was so sure of her husband's new invention that one summer morning in 1888, she packed up a motorwagen and with their two young sons made the first road trip in history. The 100-kilometre trek on rough roads took the entire day. Gasoline was used as a cleaning agent back then so it was only available at some pharmacies. Since Bertha's motorwagen could only travel only a few kilometres per tank, she made many stops for fuel along the way. Her first stop was at the City Pharmacy in Weisloch, near Heidelberg in northern Germany, which still operates as a pharmacy today and is known as the world's first gas station. Bertha only had to stop once at a blacksmith to repair one of the motorwagen's two chains. Once at her destination after a long day of travel, Bertha sent Karl a celebratory telegram. Bertha understood the value of marketing and through word of mouth and newspaper articles, the news of her remarkable journey quickly spread. The long voyage in a motorised car was the first of its kind and people were astonished to hear it was made by a woman who was simply driving her children to visit their grandmother. As the first financier of an auto manufacturer and the industry's first test driver and publicist, Bertha Benz, a Victorian-era woman, is considered the mother of the automobile.

THE REBIRTH OF THE CAR

By the end of the 1800s, ever-increasing numbers of people migrated from remote rural areas to the hustle and bustle of big cities. With horses as the primary source of transportation, the population of horses swelled and created a new problem; horse pollution. By the turn of the century, one of the primary challenges for urban planners was horse waste, as a horse typically produced a quart of urine and twenty pounds of manure a day. In 1900 the United States had 76 million people and 21 million horses—almost one horse for every four people. There were so many horses in big cities that mountains of manure were stored in empty city lots and streets were clogged with so much manure that in order to cross, people paid for the services of "crossing sweepers." The first biofuel debate was triggered when people realised the typical urban horse consumed almost 8,000 pounds of oats and hay a year which required over four acres of land — enough to feed half a dozen people. As the populations of both people and horses grew so did the competition for resources to sustain them and the opportunity for the horseless carriage was created. Gas-powered cars were loud and smoky and starting them with external hand-crank ignitions could cause severe injury. Regardless, early auto enthusiasts were thrilled at the notion of driving a machine. As popular as cars were becoming with a select few people and as unpopular as horse pollution was, the majority of people resisted cars, preferring the mode of transportation they knew. Resistance to cars was repeatedly confirmed in op-ed pieces written by companies threatened by the new beasts. Railway companies, carriage makers and horse suppliers warned of job losses and economic failure. People would suffer, they said, if the horseless carriage flourished. Ironically that same lobbying tactic of economic ruin is being used against electric cars today. In England pressure to repeal anti-car legislation grew in the 1890s as the car industry expanded around the world. In Germany, Karl Benz and Gottlieb Daimler operated companies that were developing automotive technology. Emil Jellinek, a German sportsman, raced early versions of Daimler-Benz cars and named his race team after his young daughter, Mercedes. Jellinek helped Daimler and Benz develop faster racecars and sold Mercedes cars to his wealthy friends in the racing world. Karl Benz and Gottlieb Daimler formally joined forces in 1926 and created the Daimler-Benz Company to produce cars called Mercedes Benz.

In 1896, Henry Ford was employed as an engineer with the Edison Illuminating Company where he was afforded time to work on his self-propelled vehicle, the Ford Quadricycle, which looked like its name suggested: an awkward four-wheeled motorized bicycle that he drove through the streets of Detroit. Upon meeting Henry Ford for the first time, Thomas Edison was so taken with Ford's Quadricycle that he exclaimed, "That's the thing, young man! Your car is self contained and carries its own power plant."

Ford started the Detroit Automobile Company in 1899, but poor quality and high prices hurt sales and the company closed in less than two years. Within a few months the major shareholders formed the Henry Ford Company, but when an engineer whom Ford considered a competitive threat was hired named Henry Leland, Ford left the company that bore his name. With Leland at the helm the remaining Ford Motor Company shareholders renamed the company Cadillac after the 17th century French explorer who founded the city of Detroit. In 1903 with a group of investors including machinist Horace Dodge and his financier brother John, Henry Ford formed his Ford Motor Company. Henry Leland sold Cadillac to General Motors in 1909 and the Dodge brothers went on to form their own company.

While the American automobile industry was forming what would become known as 'The Big Three' and as Daimler and Benz developed cars in Germany, a young Austrian-German engineer named Ferdinand Porsche, who had more natural genius than formal education, was working as an engineer at an electrical company in Vienna. His work caught the attention of Vienna coachbuilder, Ludwig Lohner, who hired the 23-year old Porsche to help build horseless carriages for wealthy clients. The first "Lohner-Porsche" was a two wheel-drive electric car that ran on batteries. Gas-powered motors made by Daimler were added as battery generators thereby making the Lohner-Porsche the first gasoline-electric hybrid car. Porsche would go on to form the Volkswagen and Porsche car companies.

THE RISE, FALL AND RISE OF ELECTRIC CARS

At the turn of the 20th century, electricity was still new and many people were skeptical of the mysterious technology, believing electricity would leak from plug outlets and electrical vapours would seep into the air. Kerosene lamp makers and fuel suppliers were keen to support such misguided fears in order to protect their business interests, but early enthusiasts could not be dissuaded and gladly installed electricity in their homes and businesses. Horse bus services became electrical streetcars, which popularized the notion that transportation could be powered by electricity. There were just 8,000 cars in the United States in the early 1900s. More than a third of them were electric because gas engines were not very powerful and gasoline was not readily available. Electric cars were quiet, smoke-free and starting them was far safer than hand cranking gas cars. Few people minded that electric cars could not travel long distances, because there were not many roads suitable for long distance driving.

THE FIRST NORTH AMERICAN ROAD TRIP

Horatio Nelson Jackson was a doctor who lived in Virginia, where his wealth allowed him to pursue his real passion as an adventurer. In 1903, while in San Francisco at a private men's club, he overheard a debate about whether the newfangled horseless carriage was just a passing fad. After a few drinks, Jackson slammed down $50 on a bet that he could cross the country in a horseless carriage. At the turn of the century the vast majority of people never traveled more than a dozen miles from their home in their whole lives: the distance a horse and wagon could make a round trip in one day. Horses outnumbered cars 2,500 to one. With no road signs and no road maps outside of major cities, crossing the country under any circumstance was difficult, but doing so in a horseless carriage was considered lunacy. Since he had little driving experience and no mechanical ability, Jackson hired a mechanic and co-driver, Sewall Crocker. On May 23rd 1903, just five days after making his bet, Jackson and Crocker departed San Francisco. Sixty-three days and 800 gallons of gas later, they arrived in New York City. Enormous publicity was generated throughout the journey as the press photographed and interviewed the daring duo. Fifteen years after Bertha Benz made the world's first road trip in Germany, Horatio Nelson Jackson's $50 bet fueled the imaginations of millions of Americans who began dreaming of adventures in their very own car.

FORDISM

Henry Ford founded his company the same year that Horatio Nelson Jackson made the first American road trip. In 1908, Ford launched the inexpensive and immediately popular Model T. The famous line that "Model Ts are available in any colour, as long as it's black," was less about stubbornness and more about reducing production costs. Ford introduced the moving assembly line in 1913, which further lowered production costs and in turn allowed him to lower the price of the Model-T, making it available to the giant middle-class market. In 1914, Ford doubled the pay rates for his employees which attracted the most skilled workers available, improving production efficiency and creating a new market for his cars — the people who made them. In what is sometimes referred to as Fordism, Henry Ford's manufacturing strategies democratized the automobile and made it possible for millions of people to own one. As the number of cars on the road grew, so did the availability of gasoline. Blacksmiths dealt with reduced demand for horse-related services by supplementing their income with gas sales and automobile repairs. Many of these service and gas stations added car sales to their business and became the first new-car dealers franchised by manufacturers like Ford, General Motors and Chrysler.

THE BIGGEST PUBLIC WORKS PROJECT SINCE THE PYRAMIDS

Prior to the mid-1950s, the roads in Canada and the United States were in poor condition. Canada is connected east to west by the 8,030-kilometre

Trans-Canada Highway. A group of car dealers formed the Canadian Automobile Dealer Association (CADA) in 1941 to lobby the federal government to finish paving the Trans-Canada. To this day the CADA enjoys a close relationship with the Federal Government and meets regularly with the prime minister and ministers of finance and transportation.

Construction of the U.S. interstate highway system in the 1950s was described as the world's largest public works project since the Pyramids. To complete the massive project, President Dwight Eisenhower passed the National Interstate and Defense Highways Act in 1956. At first blush connecting a highway project to military defense seems like a stretch, but Eisenhower accomplished it by appointing a long-time confidante, retired Gen. Lucius Clay, to head the committee charged with finding a way to finance the massive project. Eisenhower next appointed the CEO of General Motors, Charles Erwin Wilson, to the position of Secretary of Defense, in charge of downsizing the post-war military budget. The odd couple of the retired general working on a transportation finance plan and the auto executive working to downsize the military, built a national highway project that in today's money would cost over $200 billion. The interstate highway system was intended to create jobs, open up rural areas and provide national security for troop movement and civilian evacuation in the event of invasion or nuclear attack.

The American and Canadian highway projects literally paved the way for the North American automobile industry to begin a half-century of selling over a million cars per month.

THE SECOND COMING OF ELECTRIC CARS

The state of California alone has a population roughly equal to that of Canada with over 30 million people and almost as many cars. By the 1980s, the state's smog was reaching epidemic proportions. Under pressure from citizens demanding clean air, the state passed the Zero Emission Vehicle (ZEV) program in 1990. Under ZEV, automakers were required to produce ever-increasing percentages of their cars as ZEVs starting in 1998. General Motors acted early by introducing a prototype called the Impact at the 1990 Los Angeles Auto Show. The car was narrow at the front and rear with a rounded passenger cabin and looked a little like a spaceship from a 1950s science fiction movie. With headlights like squinting eyes and fender skirts covering the rear wheels, its look was unique and began the new automotive design trend of conspicuous conservation. In 1996 GM began producing the Impact for the public and called it the EV1. Producing over 1,000 EV1s in four years, GM made them available only through leases that specifically denied customers the ability to buy out their cars at the end of the lease. The final EV1 was produced in 1999. Inexplicably, GM began destroying the used EV1s in 2006, crushing fully functional, low-mileage cars despite protests and sit-ins by avid EV1 owners like celebrities Tom Hanks and Sylvester Stallone.

The 2006 award winning documentary, *Who Killed The Electric Car* depicted the demise of the EV1 as a whodunit mystery with a diverse list of culprits. The oil companies who had an interest in blocking alternatives were fingered, as were the automakers that prefer profitable trucks and SUVs to efficient-technology investment. The federal government's close ties with Big Oil were also cited. The film featured Chelsea Sexton, who began working on the EV1 program in 1996 and left in 2001 to co-found Plug-In America and become one of the world's best-known electric vehicle advocates. One of the scenes in the film of particular interest to me [Mike] as a car dealer involved Chelsea and her husband Bob, an electric vehicle technician, discussing electric car maintenance. With no internal

Trevor Greene and Mike Velemirovich

combustion engine, transmission or exhaust system, EVs require very little maintenance. While on a dealer trip to Los Angeles in 2008, I had dinner with Chelsea and Bob where we discussed the servicing of electric cars. As a mechanic who began his career working on internal combustion engines and went on to specialize in electric vehicles, Bob was clear on the advantages of EVs: "No oil changes. No filters for fuel or air. No mufflers. No transmission fluid. No timing belts. And no spark plugs." This means a massive reduction in business for car dealers, since labour and sales of parts represent the largest portion of profits for car dealers. This sort of bad news may cause car dealers to resist electric cars in the same way horse and buggy salesmen resisted motorcars a century ago. You can almost smell the fossil-fueled lobby campaigns. What is bad news for dealers is good news for consumers because less maintenance means significant savings for EV owners. Bob went on to explain that charging an electric car costs about 80 per cent less than fueling a conventional car. Despite the combined savings in fuel and maintenance costs, electric cars remain a tough sell for a lot of people. When I asked Chelsea why she thought that was, she cited inertia and fear of change. "Awareness is key, since many people simply do not know what EVs are, never mind their benefits," she said. Then she blew my mind by saying that about half the people who buy EVs go on to buy solar panels for home use. This points to the promise of a future where car owners actively liberate themselves from the tyranny of dependence on oil.

ELECTRIFICATION GOES MAINSTREAM

GM wasn't the only company to recognize what the Zero Emission Vehicle legislation meant to the auto industry. Toyota debuted a prototype of their Prius hybrid at the 1995 Tokyo Auto Show and launched the car for sale in Japan in 1997. A hybrid is a car with two motors that can each drive the wheels. Hybrids have a conventional gas motor and an electric motor that is recharged by both the gas motor and by regenerative braking which means as the brakes are engaged, the battery pack is recharged. Honda launched its hybrid, the Insight, in Japan in 1999. With fender skirts hiding the rear wheels, the Insight was clearly patterned after GM's EV1. Ironically, at the turn of the millennium as GM was winding down production of its plug-in electric EV1, Honda and Toyota raced to launch hybrids in America. The Japanese auto manufacturers had the foresight to recognize the electrification of the automobile was at hand. The 2006 launch of *Who Killed The Electric Car* jolted the auto industry. In the year following the documentary, Toyota Prius sales jumped almost 70 per cent and seriously embarrassed GM who quickly came up with the Chevrolet Volt, a plug-in hybrid electric vehicle much like Toyota's Prius. But unlike the Prius, the gas motor is designed only to recharge the battery, which extends the driving range of the car. The Volt was debuted at the 2007 Detroit Auto Show and immediately became a worldwide sensation.

TESLA MOTORS

Who Killed The Electric Car featured a new electric car company called Tesla Motors. The company was named after Nikola Tesla, who patented the components required for AC power in the late 1800s. South African Elon Musk founded Tesla Motors in 2003. After earning degrees in economics and physics, Musk moved to Silicon Valley in 1995, to capitalize on the dawn of the Internet. Capitalize he did, co-founding Zip2, which was acquired in 1999 by Compaq for $340 million. Next was PayPal, founded in 1998 and acquired in 2002 by eBay for $1.5 billion. One of the main reasons Musk created Tesla Motors was to combat global warming with affordable electric cars that would transform the auto industry and change the way people think about driving. Tesla entered the market with a splash in 2006, debuting a luxury sports car called the Roadster. With two seats and an electric motor that propelled the car from zero to sixty in under four seconds, the Roadster made headlines around the world. The $100,000 price tag made the Roadster unaffordable for most people, but with a range of almost 400 kilometres on a single charge, Tesla made great strides toward proving the viability of the modern electric car. I [Mike] visited the Tesla sales office in Toronto in 2011 to test drive a Roadster and I will never forget the breathtaking acceleration. In my three decades in the car business, I have driven some of the fastest cars in the world from Porsche 911s to Chevy Corvettes. But I have never experienced the neck-snapping exhilaration of launching a Tesla Roadster from zero to way over the speed limit in the blink of an eye without burning a drop of gas. In the five years following the Roadster's 2008 launch, Tesla sold over 2,400 units, which is an impressive statistic given that the car is classified as a supercar, meaning limited production and an extremely high price. Since production was stopped to change the production line to the next model, used Roadsters are in high demand and are already gaining in value, which is very rare in the car business.

The new Tesla is the Model S, a premium sedan priced lower than a Roadster. Tesla launched the Model S sedan in June 2012 to immediate success. The Model S is a low-slung, four-door sedan with an aggressive modern design described by many reviewers as the most beautiful car in the world. Motor Trend magazine named the Model S the 2013 car of the year. It was the first car of the year without an internal combustion engine in the 64-year history of Motor Trend, which declared, "At its core, the Tesla Model S is simply a damned good car you happen to plug in to refuel." Consumer Reports called the Model S the best car it ever tested and gave it their highest score: 99 out of 100. The base price of the car is C$79,000. In August 2013, the Model S was awarded a five-star safety rating by the National Traffic Safety Administration "not just overall, but in every subcategory without exception." Next will be a small SUV and finally an inexpensive electric car for the mass market.

OUTSELLING THE HEAVYWEIGHTS

By the first quarter of 2013 the Model S had outsold the full-size luxury model sedans made by Mercedes, BMW and Audi, and more impressively it sold the same volumes as the much lower-priced Chevy Volt and Nissan's plug-in electric Leaf. By the second quarter, Tesla had turned its first-ever profit, which pushed its share value over $100 and again drew worldwide attention. Despite Tesla's success, advocates for fossil fuels and the conventional auto industry insist on nay saying Tesla similar to the neighing of the horse and buggy advocates of a century ago.

SPANNING THE CONTINENT BY SUPERCHARGER

The primary objection to electric cars is range anxiety, which is worry about the limited distance an EV driver can go on a single charge. It is the main deterrent to buying an EV despite the fact that the vast majority of people drive less than fifty kilometres a day. Cars tend to be parked at home 95 per cent of the time, which means they can be recharged with inexpensive nighttime electricity. Public charging stations are popping up all over the world with more than 7,000 in the United States alone. Some of these recharging stations sell the electricity, but many are installed and funded by utility companies and governments providing free electric to early adopters. Charging away from home also presents opportunities for employers offering staff incentives to go electric and for shopping centres and restaurants to win customers with free charging stations.

Trevor Greene and Mike Velemirovich

The range for a Tesla Model S is just over 400 kilometres, made possible by its unusually large battery. Elon Musk solved the range anxiety dilemma with a series of supercharger stations powered in part by solar panels. Superchargers allow Model S owners to receive a half-charge in 20 minutes, adding about 200 kilometres to their range. By early 2014, Tesla installed enough charging stations throughout North America to allow Tesla owners to drive from Vancouver to San Diego, from Maine to Miami or from New York to Los Angeles without worrying about battery range. There is no fuel cost along the way, because Musk is committed to making superchargers free for all Tesla owners.

On January 20, 2014, Jim Glenney and his daughter Jill departed New York in a Model-S and arrived in Los Angeles on January 25. They only used Tesla's free Supercharger stations and stopped just 28 times to refuel; the number of bathroom and snack stops you would expect on a six-day cross-country trip.

For those drivers in a rush, swapping their empty battery for a fully charged unit will be an option. In June 2013, Tesla demonstrated how a Model S battery could be swapped in less time than it takes to refuel with gasoline. While supercharger stations will be free for Tesla owners, the battery-swap service will come with a fee roughly equivalent to a tank of gas. The auto industry flourished a half century ago after North America spent billions to construct a network of highways that spanned the continent. There are thousands of gas stations along the way selling fuel subsidized by billions of dollars. Elon Musk had the foresight to build his own continent-wide network of refueling stations, which should allow electric cars to flourish.

Trevor Greene and Mike Velemirovich

THE MOTHER OF INVENTION

FIGHTING GLOBAL WARMING WITH FAMILY PLANNING
Family planning in the developing world is the cheapest and most effective way to fight global warming, according to a study by a UK think tank. The Optimum Population Trust says every six dollars spent on contraception in developing nations would save one tonne of carbon dioxide emissions. Fewer babies means less need for food, shelter and prohibitively expensive health care. In real world terms, preventing one unwanted birth in a developing country would offset the 10 tonnes of carbon emitted by a return flight from England to Australia. The UN estimates that we need almost 1.3 earths to provide for all 6.8 billion of us. The global population grows by almost 84 million a year, or a new country the size of Germany. British broadcaster and naturalist, Sir David Attenborough, ignited a firestorm of controversy in January 2013 when he told the UK's Radio Times that humans are threatening their own existence and that the only way to save the planet from famine and species extinction is to limit human population growth. Attenborough, who is patron of the Optimum Population Trust, had harsh words for humanity; "We are a plague on the Earth. It's coming home to roost over the next 50 years or so. It's not just climate change; it's sheer space, places to grow food for this enormous horde. Either we limit our population growth or the natural world will do it for us, and the natural world is doing it for us right now." This statement provoked thousands of comments in the press,

mostly in this vein; "kill yourself, you desiccated, necrotic, bottom feeder. Funny how all these humans who think the world needs to rid itself of people haven't done a thing to start the ball rolling."

Educating the third world about birth control is critical. Desperately poor people keep having multiple children to take care of them. All those kids grow up physically and mentally malformed and the gene pool gets shallower and shallower. The ruling class becomes inferior and unable to lead countries competently or innovate. Fewer babies mean access to better nutrition and quality education that gives rise to a passionate and inventive generation. Good nutrition and education are rare in Africa, but some young Africans just choose to ignore the odds stacked against them and think big.

WINDMILLS, LION LIGHTS AND PEEPOWER

When he was just 14, William Kamkwamba invented a windmill for his family in drought-stricken Malawi in western Africa. Kamkwamba studied an eighth grade textbook called *Using Energy* and gathered PVC pipe, a tractor fan, a bicycle frame and blue gum tree branches to build a windmill for his subsistence-farmer parents and six sisters. In 2008, Kamkwamba was selected for the inaugural class at the African Leadership Academy in South Africa, which mentors and trains bright young Africans with leadership potential. Kamkwamba was the subject of an award-winning documentary, *Moving Windmills*, which came out in 2010, the same year he entered Dartmouth College on a scholarship. William's case is similar to Kenyan Chris Mburu, the subject of an award-winning documentary, *A Small Act*, which tells the story of how a kind Swedish woman, Hilde Back, funded Mburu's education throughout the notoriously unforgiving Kenyan secondary school system, which few poor families can afford. University is free in Kenya for the few who manage to make it that far. Mburu went on to Harvard Law School and became a UN human rights lawyer. These two young men succeeded despite crushing poverty and little opportunity and prove that the next generation of third world leaders is ready and in need of opportunity and mentorship.

Four African schoolgirls are following in William Kamkwamba's footsteps. Fourteen-year old Duro-Aina Adebola, Akindele Abiola, Faleke Oluwatoyin and 15-year old Bello Eniola unveiled a urine-powered generator on November 11, 2012 at the same trade fair, the Maker Faire, that Kamkwamba showed off his windmill. The girls' generator can produce six hours of electricity on only one litre of urine.

Richard Turere, a 13-year old Maasai schoolboy from Kenya, invented a novel gadget to prevent lions from killing his father's cows. One night he was walking around with a flashlight and discovered that lions are scared of a moving light. That gave him an idea. Richard scavenged radio parts to rig a few simple wires and light bulbs together to create a machine that would flash a series of lights, tricking the lions into thinking people were walking around with flashlights. The only thing he bought was a solar panel, which charges a battery that supplies power to the lights at night. He calls the system "Lion Lights." Richard's invention spread all around Kenya and next door in Tanzania and Zambia. They have gone overseas too: Lion Lights are being tested in India for tigers.

When Kelvin Doe was only 13, he started creating batteries and generators using materials he picked out of the trash or found around his house in Freetown, Sierra Leone. Kelvin broadcasts news and plays music as DJ Focus from his community radio station that is powered by a generator created from parts he found in the trash. When he was 16, Kelvin became the youngest person ever to be invited to the Visiting Practitioner's Program at the Massachusetts Institute of Technology.

THE GREEN BUSINESS PLAN

MAGIC MUSHROOMS

Eben Bayer and Gavin McIntyre are working magic with mushrooms. After earning degrees in mechanical engineering and product design in 2007, the pair came up with a new process for binding particles using mushrooms, creating materials that could replace Styrofoam. The first product brought out by the 26-year olds was flip-flops that are 100 per cent biodegradable. Bayer and McIntyre founded a company called Evocative Design, which uses mushroom spores as the main raw material. Their business goal is to create a viable, eco-friendly alternative to the plastics industry. They particularly have in their sights set on that toxic landfill-clogger, polystyrene, the ingredient in Styrofoam cups and packing peanuts. Dow Chemical invented Styrofoam as a thermal insulator in the 1940s. The company hollowly boasts that there isn't a coffee cup, cooler or packaging material in the world that isn't made from Styrofoam. Around 1.5 tonnes of stubbornly non-biodegradable Styrofoam is sent to landfills every day.

In a week to 10 days, Evocative Design can grow miles of super-thin, super-grippy mushroom fibre that can be molded into nearly any shape. "The products literally grow themselves. In the dark. With little to no human contact," says McIntyre. One of their early products is Greensulate, an organic, fire-resistant board made of water, flour, oyster mushroom spores and a mineral found in potting soil called Perlite. Bayer and McIntyre say the product will be as good as most insulation brands out there. It has an R-value — which is the measure of its ability to resist heat flow — of 2.9. The R-values of commercial fibreglass insulation are typically between 2.7 and 3.7.

DIAPERS FOR LUNCH

Oyster mushrooms feed on cellulose, the main material used in disposable diapers. The mushrooms have enzymes that break down cellulose, which is why they make for artsy pictures growing on dead trees in the forest. That property also makes them ideal for a less esthetically pleasing role: breaking down soiled disposable diapers in landfills. Cultivating oyster mushrooms on the gooey poop packages breaks down 90% of the diaper within two months. Within four, they are rich soil.

Phosphate is a critical component of soil but reserves are rapidly being depleted and some countries are now stockpiling phosphate to feed their populations in the future, according to Ian Sanders of the University of Lausanne, Switzerland. Some mushrooms acquire and store nutrients, specifically phosphate, and make it available to plants, acting as an extension of the plants' root systems. Scientists are producing large amounts of the fungus in high concentrations in a gel for easy transportation. From experiments on potatoes in Colombia, Sanders discovered the gel could produce the same potato crop yield as conventional methods with less than half the amount of phosphate fertilizers.

OIL AND URANIUM FOR SUPPER

Paul Stamets is an unlikely mushroom expert. He started his career in the forest as a logger, not as a scientist, and holds only a bachelor's degree. Still, Stamets has published three of the most widely read books on growing and using fungi, and in 1980 founded Fungi Perfecti, a 37-employee company that sells mushroom products and develops technological applications of mushrooms for environmental applications. Stamets had a hunch that mushrooms could soak up oil, so in 1997 he teamed up with a team of Washington state researchers to conduct experiments using mushrooms to break down diesel-contaminated soil. They found that after two months, the mushrooms had removed 97 per cent of a heavy chemical that other methods had consistently failed to break down.

THE HARVESTERS

A new breed of business organization has been born. Harvesters are companies whose sustainability-related actions and decisions add to their bottom line. Harvesters are three times more likely to have a business case for sustainability than conventional firms. And there is a high likelihood that a chief sustainability officer has a place at the board table. "A typical sustainability officer is not a lone wolf espousing some marginal position that others within the organization can choose (or not choose) to listen to. These positions have the backing of CEOs," one report said. As of September 2011, it noted that there were chief sustainability officers at 29 publicly traded companies like DuPont Chemicals, Coca Cola, AT&T and Kellogg. Sportswear giant Puma has embraced the importance of sustainability to the extent that in 2011 it became the first large company to develop an environmental profit and loss statement. Puma valued the environmental impact of its operations and supply chain at about $190 million, factoring in impacts like water use, greenhouse gas emissions, land use conversion, air pollution and waste.

A Brazilian cosmetics company called Natura is choosing its suppliers by their environmental footprints. Like Puma, Natura estimates the financial cost of their environmental impact. By reflecting these impacts into product costs, the company is able to select the suppliers that not only deliver the most cost-effective product, but also have the lowest environmental impact.

FIRST COUNTRY OFF THE GRID

The tiny island nation of Tokelau became the first in the world to be fully powered by renewable energy in 2012. Tokelau is equidistant from Hawaii and New Zealand. Most of the 1,400 residents on its three atolls farm the 10 square kilometres of land, much of which is only a few metres above sea level at high tide. A system of solar panels, storage batteries and generators running on biofuel derived from coconuts generate enough electricity to meet 150 per cent of the islands' power demand. The New Zealand government provided funding. With the flip of a switch at the end of October 2012, Tokelau went from being completely dependent on imported fuels to being completely energy independent in one of the largest off-grid renewable energy projects in the world.

GOD DOESN'T THINK HE'S LARRY ELLISON

Massive fortunes tend to bring out either a generous nobility or a base vindictiveness in people. There are noble billionaires who are spending their massive wealth on projects that will hopefully cancel out the environmental crimes of the vindictive mega-rich.

Most people go to Hawaii. Oracle CEO Larry Ellison bought it. In the summer of 2012, Ellison bought most of Lanai; 141 square miles of virtually untouched island paradise southwest of Honolulu with one school, 3,200 people and only 30 miles of pavement. Ellison wants to turn his island into a "model for sustainable enterprise." Electric cars will rule the road, the sun and wind will power the island and the organic farms will be watered with fresh water converted from seawater. James Dole, the founder of Dole Foods, bought Lanai in 1922. Most of the pineapple groves on the island are abandoned. There is a strain of tree that Ellison would do well to consider for his tired pineapple groves. Pongam trees are drought-resistant evergreens that grow to about 40 feet. On average, one hectare of Pongam trees can absorb 30 tons of carbon per year. Pongams are the Swiss army knives of the woods. The seedpods from the beautiful lavender blossoms produce everything from medicines, soap and antiseptics to insect repellent, dyes and lubricants. Pongoms seem to have been designed as a source of biofuel; they grow up to 40 feet tall, thrive on marginal lands like abandoned pineapple groves, require little water, are pest-resistant and don't need fertilizer. Our Larry has always lived large as the world's fifth richest billionaire with a net worth estimated at $55 billion. Ellison founded his business software company, Oracle Corp., with $1,200 in 1977. He won the 2010 America's Cup sailing race and his first biography is titled *The Difference Between God and Larry Ellison: God Doesn't Think He's Larry Ellison.* Ellison's former yacht, Rising Sun, is the 11th largest in the world. Apparently, in a "mine is bigger" moment, Ellison specifically designed the yacht to be larger than Microsoft co-founder Paul Allen's. But, at 452 feet long and five stories tall, the Rising Sun is too big to come alongside most marinas. Apparently, mooring out with the oil tankers and tendering in to shore was cramping Larry's style, so he commissioned a new, presumably smaller, yacht to be built in Europe.

WAGING WAR ON CARBON

Larry Ellison isn't the only billionaire trying to fund a sustainable future. Sir Richard Branson founded the Carbon War Room (CWR) in early 2009. He brought together 15 other high-powered entrepreneurs from around the world to figure out how to make the business case for carbon dioxide reduction and sustainable energy development attractive for entrepreneurs. The CWR took a page from Larry Ellison's idea of converting Lanai into a model for sustainable development in June 2012 when it joined the Caribbean island of Aruba in an attempt to go to 100 per cent renewable energy and create the world's second sustainable country by 2020.

CALLING THE CARBON BUBBLE

Jeremy Grantham is a wildly successful fund manager and a dedicated behind-the-scenes supporter of environmental causes: the Oz figure of the environmental movement. He became a legend in the financial world for predicting all the major stock market bubbles of recent decades. Grantham made big money for his clients and himself until the mid-1990s when he went on holiday with his children to the Amazon and Borneo. "And without thinking about it, you start talking about the logs along the side of the river and the lack of mature forests in Borneo," he told a magazine. The man who made a fortune pegging all the major ups and downs of an unpredictable market, has made a call on the most critical market of them all: our environment. Grantham says some investors shy away from recognising market trends with head-in-the-sand reactions to some environmental challenges. "In a bull market you want to believe good news," he says. "You don't want to hear that the market is going to go off a cliff." Grantham says climate skeptics are guided by ideology and choose to ignore the obvious effects of climate change, like Superstorm Sandy. "They have profound beliefs — as opposed to knowledge — that they are willing to protect by all manner of psychological tricks. So you have people who are very smart like great analysts and hedge-fund managers who on paper know that their argument is wrong, but who promote it fiercely because they are libertarians," he said.

Trevor Greene and Mike Velemirovich

"They are using incredible ingenuity to steer their way around facts they do not choose to accept." Grantham is hopeful for the future, and as he did with all of his predictions, he backs it up with facts. "The business mathematics of alternative energy are changing much faster [than many people] realise." Grantham thinks higher carbon taxes along with "the increasing affordability of alternative energy, will mean that coal and oil from tar sands run the very substantial risk of being stranded assets."

CHINESE CAVALRY

Grantham looks to the east for salvation. "China is my secret weapon. The Chinese cavalry riding to the rescue." He has high hopes for China "because they have embedded high scientific capabilities in their leadership class. They know this is serious. And they are acting much faster now than we are," he says. "They have it within their capabilities to come back in 30 years with the guarantee of complete energy independence – all alternative and sustainable forever." Grantham says the massive amount of capital in China is the key. But Grantham thinks that is no excuse for the perennially capital-challenged West to just give up. "Anyone who says government can't do this, or can't do that, I say a pox on you; have a look at the [atomic bomb] Manhattan Project. They did remarkable things. They stuck the brightest minds out in the desert. They were herding cats with great egos, but it worked. If we did that on alternative energy, we'd be home free."

Trevor Greene and Mike Velemirovich

THE AGE OF THE "TERRARIST"

Journalist Tom Englehart wrote an incisive essay in the investigative journalism magazine, Mother Jones, in May 2013 in which he noted that there are words like genocide for the destruction of a racial or ethnic group. Ecocide describes the destruction of the environment. But, he notes, there isn't a word for the ruin of the Earth and suggests "terracide" from the Latin word for earth. Englehart identifies the CEOs of energy giants such as Exxon, BP and Shell as terrarists. "You can take one thing for granted: not a single terrarist will ever go to jail, and yet they certainly knew what they were doing. *You're the one who's going to pay, especially your children and grandchildren.*" At the ExxonMobil AGM in May 2013, Exxon CEO Rex Tillerson said that an economy that runs on oil is here to stay and that cutting carbon emissions would do no good. The king of the terrarists, who made $34.9 million in 2011, asked his acolytes a rhetorical question: "What good is it to save the planet if humanity suffers?" The assembled Exxon faithful then went on to defeat, for the seventh time, by a margin of three-to-one, resolutions to reduce greenhouse gas emissions. Tillerson seems to think humankind can engineer its way out of any climate crisis: "as a species that's why we're all still here: We have spent our entire existence adapting. So we will adapt to this. It's an engineering problem, and it has engineering solutions. In 2013, Tillerson told "My philosophy is to make money," Tillerson said, "If I can drill and make money, then that's what I want to do."

Englehart muses, "If the oil execs aren't terrarists, then who is? And if that doesn't make the big energy companies criminal enterprises, then how would you define that term? To destroy our planet with malice aforethought, with only the most immediate profits on the brain, with only your own comfort and well being (and those of your shareholders) in mind: Isn't that the ultimate crime? Isn't that terracide?"

THE KINGS OF GREED

There's a Buddhist quote about greed that goes far to explain the behaviour of the terrarists; *the five desires (wealth, lust, fame, food and sleep) are like brine—the more you drink the thirstier you become. Our greed is as deep as the ocean; you can never get to the bottom of it.* One of mega-rich industrialist David Koch's first contributions to the American democratic process was in 1980 when he ran for vice president on the Libertarian Party ticket. One of his more recent contributions came in 2012 when he spent millions trying to buy the US presidency for the doomed Mitt Romney. Koch, who is worth $31 billion, has a pet political organization, Americans for Prosperity (AFP). In December 2012 the AFP told Congress not to vote for a federal aid package for victims of Hurricane Sandy, warning on its website that "Americans for Prosperity will include this vote in our congressional scorecard." Which means legislators who vote for the bill risk a torrent of attack ads in their next election. Koch's man in New Jersey, Steve Lonegan, called the aid package a disgrace. "This is not a federal government responsibility," Lonegan told reporters. "We need to suck it up and be responsible for taking care of ourselves." There are four Koch brothers but the oldest, Fred, and the youngest, Bill, aren't involved in the business. Charles and David are, respectively, chairman and executive vice president of Koch Industries. They rule an empire that spews 100 million tons of carbon every year into the air we breathe. Since 1997, these beauties have secretly funneled $61.5 million to climate change-denial groups. They also gave millions to the far right-wing Tea Party to fight President Obama's health care reform. One of the world's largest privately held conglomerates, Koch Industries has its talons in timber, oil refining, ethanol production, chemicals, pipelines, consumer products and fertilizer. In the Spring 2012 issue of Massachusetts-based *CommonWealth* magazine, David Koch discussed his opposition to a controversial wind farm, Cape Wind, off Cape Cod. Koch matter-of-factly admits he has spent millions to block the project because he doesn't want to ruin the view from his Cape Cod waterfront estate. He called the project "visual pollution" and said he "was buying more property on the Cape for a family compound and the windmills would interfere with the aesthetics." Koch has been the main donor — reportedly at least $1.5 million — to the Alliance to Protect Nantucket Sound, a group with the sole mandate of stopping the Cape Wind project. It's all in vain though, because Cape Wind already has the federal and state permits it needs, has sold over 75 per cent of its electricity, and has $2 billion borrowed from the Bank of Tokyo-Mitsubishi to play with. The Cape Wind plan was dealt a major setback in January 2015 when two power companies that had agreed to buy energy from the Nantucket Sound wind farm terminated their contracts with the developers, raising questions about the future of the $2.5 billion offshore project. Advances in the state's renewable energy and efficiency policies have lessened the importance of Cape Wind in its overall energy landscape, Bowles said.

DIRTY, DIRTY LAUNDRY

A February 2013 piece in *The Independent* reads like a page from a Dan Brown novel. It breathlessly reported on a shadowy group called The Donors Trust, a secretive US funding organization that enables its billionaire clients to anonymously donate hundreds of millions to climate change denial groups. Another Koch creation is a so-called "corporate bill mill" known as the American Legislative Exchange Council [ALEC], which pushes "model bills" such as mandating the teaching of climate change denial in public school systems. Budding deniers started being brainwashed in Louisiana and Texas in 2009, South Dakota the next year and Tennessee in 2013.

THE ANTI-KOCH

California billionaire Tom Steyer retired from running the $19 billion hedge fund he founded to devote himself full time to the environmental cause. Steyer, the 347th richest person in the US, is dedicating his fortune to fighting climate change through political donations to politicians who share his green views. Steyer isn't shy about his plans to "destroy" climate skeptics and his stated aim to score a "smashing victory" over them. Steyer got stuck into the Massachusetts special Senate election of June 2013 by targeting fellow Democrat, Stephen Lynch, for his pro-Keystone XL pipeline stance. Steyer sent Lynch a letter threatening an aggressive PR campaign against him because of Lynch's support for the pipeline. On March 22nd 2013, Steyer wrote "because climate change is such a serious issue, and because it is on the ballot as never before, we are asking you, Congressman Lynch, today to do one of two things by high noon on Friday, March 22. Either act like a real Democrat and oppose Keystone's dirty energy. Or, get a sworn, binding statement — with securities law enforcement — from TransCanada and the refiners that all of the Keystone-shipped oil will stay here." Steyer wanted to get the other Democrat, Edward Markey elected. Markey is of course opposed to the Keystone. An unruffled Lynch voted in May 2013 in favour of a bill to fast track the pipeline.

FLAT-OUT DENIAL

Through all recorded history only a few dozen people have been fortunate enough to travel into space and gaze upon the spinning blue orb that is Planet A. To the other 100 billion humans who have ever lived on Earth, our world appears to be flat with the sun revolving around us at what feels like the center of the universe. Today, despite hundreds of space flights, thousands of photographs and countless scientific confirmations, the Flat Earth Society has a thriving membership with a well-organized social media campaign. They even have an online gift shop. Flat Earthers steadfastly believe Earth is flat with the universe spinning around us and passionately deny all evidence to the contrary as elaborate conspiracy theories. But they are an innocuous, polite lot who appear to have little to gain from their denial of science except perhaps the odd online t-shirt sale.

Science denial was taken to a frighteningly low point in western culture by the response of the major tobacco companies to the 1964 American Surgeon General's report proving the negative health effects of smoking. During the three decades that followed, Big Tobacco engaged in a relentless campaign of disinformation while more than 12 million people died in North Ame ica alone from smoking-related diseases. Organizations with lofty n like the Center for Indoor Air Research and the Council for Tobac search popped up, which were little more than public relations f fake credentials to mislead the public. A favourite tactic w *impartial* research into *allegations* that cigarettes were h plication being that the scientific research of the day wa The industry was highly motivated to deny science, b billions of dollars. In 1994, the CEOs of seven r corporations appeared before Congress and test cigarette smoking leads to cancer and heart dis

166

Trevor Greene and Mike Velemirovich

went on to claim that cigarettes are not addictive and that they did not advertise to children. Just weeks later, documents from tobacco giant Brown and Williamson were delivered to the University of California revealing that the tobacco industry had full knowledge that cigarettes were addictive and caused fatal disease. Whistleblower, Dr. Jeffry Wigand, who in 1994 had headed Brown and Williamson's research and development division, went on the television show *60 Minutes* to tell the world Big Tobacco had full knowledge of just how lethal and addictive cigarettes are. Since then tobacco companies have grudgingly admitted to the dangers of smoking as they pay billions of dollars in lawsuits around the world. Wigand, who was portrayed by actor, Russell Crowe, in the 1999 movie *The Insider,* runs a non profit called Smoke Free Kids, which helps kids make healthy choices about tobacco use.

AN INSIDIOUS CIRCLE OF DENIAL

Given the massive lawsuits faced by tobacco companies one would think corporations would be more careful in responding to scientific research, but sadly that is not the case. Human-influenced climate change has been proven by thousands of scientists working independently around the world and yet deniers persist. Unlike the tobacco wars where one industry desperately tried to protect its single business interest, climate change denial is much more complicated, because there are so many more factors involved. Leading the charge on denying climate change are the fossil fuel industries. Following a close second are the industries that burn fuel such as public utilities, manufacturers and transportation companies. The final and most crucial people denying climate change are the politicians whose very livelihood depend on the financial support of the first two sets of deniers. This devious circle of denial is more insidious than science denial by the tobacco industry, because tobacco simply kills users, whereas climate change deniers jeopardize every living thing on Earth — an Earth some swear is flat.

MACTRUMP THE MEANIE

In March 2013, the Scottish government gave the green light to its most controversial wind project proposal. It wasn't controversial because it was near an environmentally sensitive area so unique that it has been called "Scotland's Amazon." The European Offshore Wind Deployment Centre project was controversial because Donald Trump was involved, waving his money and mane around and being his usual understated, reasonable self. Trump claimed that the proposed project near Aberdeen would ruin the scenic coastal views from his new golf course project, and that "the reckless installation of these monsters will single-handedly have done more damage to Scotland than virtually any event in Scottish history." He asserted that the wind farm would cause the "destruction of Scotland's coastline." Unperturbed, Energy Minister Fergus Ewing gave approval for the project in April 2012, which will produce enough to power almost half of Aberdeen's 100,000 homes. Scotland has set an ambitious mandate to achieve a 100 per cent renewable power supply by 2020. Trump accepted the defeat with his customary grace: "it will be like looking through the bars of a prison and the Scottish citizens will be the prisoners," the Donald whinnied. "Luckily, tourists will not suffer because there will be none as they will be going to other countries that had the foresight to use other forms of energy." Then Trump made his most outrageous comment of all; "I am doing this to save Scotland."

YOU'VE BEEN TRUMPED

Trump International Golf Links opened in July 2012. Sprawling over a thousand acres are two 18-hole golf courses, a 450-room hotel and 1,500 luxury homes in a residential village. Trump's much-hyped course was largely empty for a time after opening, as if the witches from Shakespeare's *Macbeth* had put a curse on it. If tourists wanted to go, they had to make their own way to and from the star-crossed place, because the guided golf tour companies would not deal with Trump's collection of holes. One visitor had harsh words on the travel website Trip Advisor: "this place has totally devastated the local land and wildlife as well as life for many of the locals. Please consider this before lining Trump's pockets."

A documentary film told entirely without narration was made about the whole tragic saga. *You've Been Trumped* won critical acclaim and awards all over the world and was named top Scottish feature film in 2011. The film showed how Trump tried to bully the farmers and fishermen in nearby Balmedie, a town of 3,000, into selling their property. When farmer, Michael Forbes, refuses to sell, Trump declares his farm a slum and a pigsty. Forbes loses his electricity and water and huge mounds of dirt and sand appear near the village. The area, described by one environmentalist as a fragile and irreplaceable "mosaic of habitats," and the "crown jewels of Scotland's natural heritage," was transformed into a muddy construction site. Blinded by Trump's claims that over 6,000 jobs will be created in the economically depressed region, the authorities made no effort to support the residents. Trump was awarded an honorary degree in business administration in 2010 from Aberdeen's Robert Gordon University, which prompted a previous honoree, the Scottish environmentalist David Kennedy, to return his degree.

EARTH, WIND AND FIRE

THE OZONE VICTORY

Scientists in the Antarctic began monitoring the ozone layer in the late 1950s. In 1985, they'd determined that since the mid-1970s the ozone layer had been steadily decreasing. The ozone layer is at the lower part of the stratosphere, about 20 kilometres above Earth and absorbs much of the sun's ultraviolet radiation. The scientists found that chlorofluorocarbons [CFCs] from aerosol sprays were rising into the stratosphere where they were destroying ozone molecules. A depleted ozone shield layer would allow more dangerous UV rays to reach the Earth's surface, likely causing skin cancer epidemics and cataracts. From its discovery in 1979 to 1987 the hole in the Antarctic ozone layer grew to 22 million square kilometres. In the 1980s, concern over diminishing ozone led to apocalyptic theorizing and images came out of people swathed head to toe under a blazing sky. The media was filled with warnings about CFCs and at a time when big hairdos were fashionable, aerosol cans were demonized. CFCs were a component of vehicle air conditioning until 1994 when auto manufacturers went completely CFC-free. Four years earlier, people who bought Volkswagens without air conditioning could have their cars retrofitted with cooling units that used CFCs or for a modest premium could choose CFC-free units. My [Mike's] dealership decided to go CFC-free and customers paid the premium to avoid the perils of ozone depletion and to participate in the promise of a cleaner world. September 2012 was the 25th anniversary of the Montreal Protocol, an international agreement to phase out CFC use with signatories from Afghanistan to Zimbabwe that saved the ozone layer, then the direst planetary crisis we faced. The doomsday scenarios were averted, the ozone layer is healing and countries have committed to phase out the last ozone-depleting chemicals. The number of countries that have complied with their Montreal commitments is unusually high. Scientists say if they continue to hold to their commitments, they expect the Antarctic ozone hole to close up for good later this century. The treaty does double duty: many ozone-depleting substances are greenhouse gases. The Montreal Protocol has been estimated to have prevented annual emissions of 13 billion tonnes of carbon dioxide. It marked a victory for civil global cooperation on an environmental threat.

EUROPE'S RECHARGEABLE BATTERY

A major problem with green power is inconsistency because the sun will inevitably stop shining and the wind has to stop blowing. The challenge is storing the power from the blazing sun and the howling wind. Norway appears to have an answer. Over 99 per cent of Norway's electricity is from hydro, mostly through pumped-storage hydroelectric power plants, which have upper and lower reservoirs. During peak times, the water flows down as usual. The idea is to use excess energy from the rest of Europe to pump the water back to the upper reservoir through a reversible turbine; a generator on the way down, a pump on the way up to be ready for peak hours or shortages. The good news is the existing hydropower system can be retrofitted with new tunnels and turbines. Norway's New Tyin plant came on line in 2004, pumping out 1,400 gigawatts an hour, enough to power 140,000 North American homes.

SWEDISH WIND

Sweden is going to follow suit with the biggest wind farm in the world. The Blekinge Wind Farm won government approval in February 2013. Seven hundred wind turbines are expected to crank out 2,500 megawatts of juice a year with construction planned for 2014 or 2015, which is enough to power 250,000 North American homes.

GREEK FIRE

Things weren't as pleasant in Greece. Since extreme austerity measures were instituted in 2010, Athens has frequently been the scene of fiery riots. Smoke from petrol bombs and tear gas regularly cast a pall over the capital, but since Athens raised the tax on heating oil by more than 400 per cent, acrid wood smoke has been in the air. Athenians have returned to the desperate ways of World War II and are burning trees from the parks, old furniture and scrap wood to stay warm. Even the remains of a 3,000 year-old olive tree, where Plato is said to have spoken beside, have gone up in smoke.

The UK's George Monbiot has been called one of the world's most influential radical thinkers. Monbiot, a best-selling author, won the UN Global 500 Award for outstanding environmental achievement. He wrote a book in 2006 that chronicles the enduring threat of overheating our Earth but, unlike the vast majority of books on the same subject, offers some solutions with a "spirit of optimism." In *Heat: How to Stop the Planet From Burning* Monbiot does not mince words: "we are the last generation that can make this happen, and this is the last possible moment at which we can make it happen." He puts his finger on the political realities that hamstring the global effort to curb climate change like self-serving and ineffective UN climate summits: "political parties in most rich nations … know that we will grumble about their failure to curb climate change, but that we will not take to the streets. They know that nobody ever rioted for austerity."

RECESSION ECONOMICS IRISH STYLE

Ireland was the first economy in the EU to plummet in the 2008 recession. But while suffering in the depths of an economic meltdown, it found a unique way to claw itself out of what the International Monetary Fund [IMF] called the most expensive and deepest bank crash of any economy since the Great Depression: they charged homes and businesses for the environmental havoc they caused by imposing a carbon tax. Prices of oil, natural gas and kerosene soared because the government taxed fossil fuels based on the carbon it emitted. Garbage was put on a diet because the household trash was weighed at the curb and residents were charged for anything that was not being recycled. But the Irish quickly learned to love renewables and recycling. The 1,100 wind turbines in operation in Ireland are set to double by 2020. The carbon tax has raised nearly $1.3 billion, which enabled the Irish government to avoid a rise in income tax rates and pay off much of the huge bailout they got from the IMF and the European Union. Ireland had been one of Europe's highest per capita producers of greenhouse gases, on a par with the US, but has steadily cut emissions since 2008 and is on track to meet its Kyoto commitments.

FLYING HIGH ON COOKING OIL

The Dutch airline, KLM, started a biofuel experiment in 2009 with flights between Amsterdam and Paris. In March 2013 it made its first biofueled jaunt over the Atlantic from Amsterdam to New York on a fuel mix of 25 per cent recycled cooking oil and 75 per cent jet fuel.

PASSIVE GERMAN HOUSES

German lawmaker, Dr. Hermann Scheer, has shaped Germany into a leader of renewable energy development. In 2000, Scheer helped pass what many think is the world's most effective renewable-energy law, the Renewable Energy Sources Act. The law requires electric utility companies to buy energy from renewable energy suppliers such as residents who have fitted their homes with solar panels, communities with wind turbines or farmers who create biofuels from manure. The city of Freiburg in southwest Germany personifies Scheer's vision. Freiburg was destroyed by bombers in the Second World War so the town burghers rebuilt using leading edge energy-saving principles. One of the cornerstones of the Freiburg energy revolution is the "passive house." Conceived by scientists in the late 1980s, a passive house is constructed with a building envelope that shields the inner living area from the outer, reducing or eliminating the need for an active heating or cooling system.

In March 2012, German solar power plants met nearly half of the country's midday electricity needs. The 22 gigawatts of electricity per hour set a world record and were equal to the power from 20 nuclear energy stations at full capacity. The timing was significant as well. Solar power generated a third of the electricity needs of one of the most highly industrialized countries on a workday, Friday, and nearly half on Saturday. The Germans have gone solar in a big way with nearly as much installed solar power generation capacity as the rest of the world combined.

TURNING TRASH INTO GOLD

Most of the greenest cities in the world are, no surprise, in Scandinavia. Perhaps the greenest of them all is Iceland's capital, Reykjavik. On the smallish side with a population of 115,000, Reykjavik has been going for green since it set up a government agency in the 1940s to learn how to harness the abundant geothermal energy of its waterfalls, geysers, volcanoes and hot springs. Today, the city gets all its energy from renewables. Iceland is also on the way towards phasing out gasoline, which can reach $8 a gallon locally, and switching to hydrogen for its city buses.

Sweden is so good at recycling garbage that it has to import the stuff. Because only four per cent of household waste in Sweden goes to municipal landfills, the remainder is recycled or burned as fuel at waste-to-energy power plants. Sweden imports 800,000 tons of trash a year from Europe, especially Norway next door. Emissions from the burning waste are a concern, as well as dioxin and heavy metals in the ashes but the heavy metals are stored in landfill and the ashes are sent back to Norway. The peculiar alchemy of sustainable energy looks poised to turn trash into gold. Oslo's 650,000 citizens don't generate enough trash to sustain its garbage-for-energy model. Oslo uses trash-incineration waste to fuel half its buildings and homes and all of its schools. It has been forced to import trash from the UK. According to *The New York Times*, northern Europe produces only about 150 million tons of waste a year, far too little to supply incinerating plants that can handle more than 700 million tons.

The rest of the world got a late start in renewables but is not far behind…

PLAYING CATCH UP TO EUROPE

NANAIMO

John Mandziuk could have been a rocket scientist. He was accepted to Caltech in 1980 for aerospace engineering but when he found out tuition alone was more than the value of his parent's home, John started a career as a Certified Management Accountant in Vancouver. That year, he volunteered at his niece's high school supervising a student-built salmon hatchery. Over dinner one night Uncle John was asked why he wasn't teaching. He eventually wound up with an education degree and a job at Wellington Secondary in Nanaimo. He turned out to be the kind of caring, cool, outside-the-box teacher that molds leaders. While on a vacation to Maui, John read an article about aquaponics and the light bulb went off. He organized his students to get funding and built an aquaponics system. They built a "green wall" of PVC piping with cutouts for plants that is attached to a 600-litre tank. A pump moves water from a fish tank through the top of the green wall. The plants get nourishment from the nitrates produced by the fish waste in the water and strip out toxic ammonia to keep the water clean. The ultimate goal is to provide fresh food for the cafeteria.

SUSTAINABILITY PARTNERS-GIBSON'S, BC

Brian Nattrass was a hotshot corporate lawyer in Calgary in the 1990s when he had an epiphany that felt like a heart attack. Nattrass had such a blazing insight about the fouled world he was leaving for his children that it compelled him to swap his pinstripes in corporate boardrooms for overalls in dumpsters behind IKEA stores in Sweden. Nattrass and his wife Mary founded a company, Sustainability Partners, that advises large companies on becoming sustainable. Their clients include Nike, Starbucks and the US Army. They basically wrote the sustainability doctrine that the army uses to develop strategy. Every year, thousands of former soldiers enter the civilian workforce with extensive experience in sustainability practices.

According to the Washington Post, military spending on renewable energy soared 300 per cent from $400 million to $1.2 billion between 2006 and 2009. And it is on track to reach more than $10 billion a year by 2030. The largest consumer of energy in the US, the Department of Defense has pledged to get 25 per cent of its energy from renewable sources by 2025. The Navy and Marine Corps plan to slash fossil fuel use in half by 2020. US Navy secretary Ray Mabus admitted in a Washington Post piece that lowering carbon emissions, "… is a good byproduct, but it's a byproduct." Mabus is mainly concerned with the fact that a Marine is either wounded or killed for every 50 convoys of fuel brought into Afghanistan.

BOGOTA

Enrique Peñalosa is a green philosopher king. In his three-year tenure as mayor of Bogota, Columbia, he overhauled the city's bike paths, saying, "A bikeway is a symbol that shows that a citizen on a $30 bicycle is equally important as a citizen in a $30,000 car." February 1st is Car-Free Day in Bogota, a reflection of Penalosa's assertion that commutes, not work itself, are what depress the workforce in a city like his. Penalosa famously said "a city can be friendly to people or it can be friendly to cars, but it can't be both," as he raised gas taxes. Eventually school enrollment shot up 30 per cent and rush hour traffic improved threefold. At the same time, for some reason, the murder rate plummeted 40 per cent.

CURITIBA

The most interesting thing about the capital of Brazil's southeastern province of Parana is that the city parks of Curitiba are trimmed by sheep. The city of 1.8 million, *Reader's Digest's* choice as the best place to live in Brazil, also boasts an excellent transit system, which in the 1970s was efficiently divided into concentric circles within commercial corridors. Fully 90 per cent of Curitibans recycle two-thirds of their trash every day and can exchange it for fresh produce.

PIPLANTRI, INDIA

In the developing world, boys are prized above girls and violence against women is endemic, as evidenced by the horrific gang rape and murder of a young Delhi nurse in late 2012. Not so in a tiny village in western India. The 8,000 villagers in Piplantri plant 111 trees every time a girl is born and her parents sign an affidavit promising that they will not marry her off before the legal age, will send her to school regularly and take care of the trees planted in her name. In the last six years, over 250,000 trees have been planted on the village's grazing commons. To keep termites away from the trees, two and a half million Aloe Vera plants were planted around them. The Aloe Vera is a source of livelihood for several residents.

NEW ORLEANS

The 2013 Super Bowl in New Orleans was the greenest one yet. Over 7,000 trees were planted in January and a New Orleans utility bought credits to offset the 4,500 megawatts of power that produced some 3.8 million pounds of carbon dioxide. The offset projects included a landfill-gas collection project in Texas, a forest conservation initiative in California and a Michigan methane-capture project. And the leftover food from nearly 50 Super Bowl events during the week leading up to the game was delivered to New Orleans food banks.

THE DRAGON KINGDOM

Bhutan, which means "land of dragons" in the local language, was ranked the happiest nation in Asia and the eighth happiest in the world in 2006. In 1971 it adopted happiness as its measure of prosperity instead of tawdry wealth. Landlocked in the Himalayan highlands between India and China, the kingdom of 800,000 souls is among the poorest and least developed countries in the world. Bhutan's very first UN resolution was to give more importance to happiness to measure social and economic development. It was passed without a vote because the happy Bhutanese delegates were able to secure the support of 68 co-sponsors. Like Ecuador, Bhutan has enshrined nature in its constitution, pledging to forever maintain 60 per cent of the country as forest and putting an outright ban on logging for export. Bhutan even bans all private vehicles for one day a month. In April 2013, Bhutan announced that it would try to become the first country in the world to become fully organic by banning the sales of pesticides and herbicides and using its own animals and farm waste for fertilisers. Pema Gyamtsho, Bhutan's minister of agriculture and forests, said most farm practices are traditional already. "But we are Buddhists, too, and we believe in living in harmony with nature. Animals have the right to live, we like to see plants happy and insects happy," he said.

HOPE FOR AFGHANISTAN

ALADDIN'S CAVE UNDER THE SAND

When I [Trevor] patrolled the Kandahar desert, I would never have guessed that I was walking over the planet's largest — by a long shot — reserves of minerals. The story of the discovery reads like an outtake from an Indiana Jones film. It starts in 2004 with a team of American geologists, probably working through a provincial reconstruction team similar to mine, who scoured the library of the Afghan Geological Survey in Kabul. They came across some old charts that indicated several large mineral deposits. The data had been collected by Soviet mining experts in the 1980s then forgotten in the 1989 withdrawal. In the 1990s, through civil war and Taliban rule, Afghan geologists took the charts home and returned them to the library in 2001 when the Taliban were dislodged from power. The United States Geological Survey used the charts in 2007 to conduct the most comprehensive geological survey of Afghanistan ever done. Finally, in 2009, business development officials from the Pentagon looked at the data and realized the economic potential of the mineral deposits. "This will become the backbone of the Afghan economy," Jalil Jumriany, an Afghan ministry of mines official told the New York Times in 2010. But there might be too many intractable obstacles to overcome before that backbone is in place. If the current war is ended with few power-sharing concessions to the Taliban, there are always the many ancient tribal conflicts that need to be resolved.

Trevor Greene and Mike Velemirovich   179

And if the prospect of huge wealth is enough to make tribes somehow find a way to co-operate, there is the endemic culture of corruption in the Karzai government that saw Afghanistan's minister of mines accept a $30 million bribe from China in 2009 for copper-mining rights. My pessimistic analysis of the obstacles to tapping the potential of this mineral wealth is inexpert and informed by the friends and colleagues I left behind in the desert. Saad Mohseni was senior economic advisor to the Afghan government from 2002 to 2004 and is an expert on the future of Afghanistan. After the Taliban were removed from power in 2001, he returned to his country with his brothers to help rebuild. The Mohseni boys set up Afghanistan's first independent media group. Arnan TOLO TV FM is the cornerstone of the MOBY Group, of which Mohseni is chairman. Arnan FM TOLO takes its name from the Dari word for "dawn" and embodies Mohseni's optimism for Afghanistan. An essay he wrote in March 2013 for the Wall Street Journal tells a much brighter, better informed story and is "influenced by my belief in the human spirit and the resilience of our people," says Mohseni, who kindly allowed us to reprint his piece:

The Untold Story of Afghan Progress

By SAAD MOHSENI

The conventional wisdom about Afghanistan runs something like this: The country is a lost cause. Almost nothing has changed. The people remain backward and thankless, and there is little benefit for the international community to stay engaged in the country's future. This is far from the truth. Despite many years of conflict, Afghanistan has exhibited dramatic signs of economic, social and cultural revival. The country has undergone such extraordinary change since 9/11 that a return to the dark period of the Taliban is unfathomable. One source of the misconception about my country is the Afghan government's combative relationship with the international community. But the government doesn't reflect the views of the public. Most people in Afghanistan remain strongly supportive of international engagement and widely approve of the presence of troops from other countries. Afghanistan is a young nation. The median age is 17, and 60 per cent of the people are under age 20. This generation is like no other in the country's history. Today, there are over eight million children enrolled in schools—and 2.6 million of those students are girls. In 2001, the nation's classrooms seated only 900,000 boys and practically no girls. The literacy rate is currently 33% and is set to grow to 60% by 2025. The country's greatest achievement is its democratic process. Many forget that Afghanistan is preparing for its third complete cycle of presidential and parliamentary elections in 2014 and 2015—thanks in part to the continued engagement of the international community. The political process, flawed at times, is nevertheless allowing the country to develop as a modern nation. Challenges remain. The corruption and ineptitude in many parts of the Afghan government, alongside the insurgency—which is widely known to be financed and orchestrated by meddling regional players—have both done much to contribute to a sense of doom and gloom, especially in the West. As for talks with the Taliban, encouraged by some in the U.S. government, they have yet to deliver anything of substance. The insurgents themselves, despite the weakness of the Kabul government, remain very unpopular. Their approval rating, measured by the BBC and by other polls over the years, has consistently come in at under 10% nationally, with less than 30% even in the Taliban heartland of Kandahar. Any peace deal with the insurgency needs to evolve organically, be led by Afghans and take into account the wishes of the majority of the people. Today's Afghanistan is a modernizing nation, connected by thousands of miles of roads, airwaves and the Internet. With all the improvements in education, health and living standards, the young men and women of my country regard the progress of the past decade as the foundation for an even brighter future. And with the selection of a new government in 2014, the people just might stay on the path they chose in 2001. The world must not give up on Afghanistan now.

TOMORROWLAND TODAY

On the way over to Afghanistan, we staged through Camp Mirage in an "unnamed country in the Middle East." We got kicked out of the United Arab Emirates in 2010 because we didn't want their planes to have extra landing rights in Canada, which cost us a base from which to acclimatize to the heat and get used to soldiering in serious dust. Up the coast from the base stands a real-world Tomorrowland. In 2007, Abu Dhabi trumpeted its plans for "the world's first zero-carbon city" on its outskirts. The futuristic city, Masdar, which means "Source City" in Arabic, was planned as a perfect square mile raised 23 feet above the desert to catch the breezes. Based on the architecture and urban planning of traditional Arab settlements, Masdar City has narrow streets, exterior walls and walkways, thick-walled buildings and courtyards. The city is powered by renewable energy and designed to create the lowest possible carbon footprint. But it's the method of transportation that really sets it apart and gives it an authentic Disneyesque touch; underneath the streets, driver-less electric cars swoosh silently through dimly lit tunnels.

Trevor Greene and Mike Velemirovich

OUTSIDE THE BOX INC.

Three University of Toronto graduates have invented a light bulb that produces as much light as a 100-watt incandescent bulb using just an eighth of the power. The "Nanolight" is billed as "the world's most energy-efficient light bulb" and garnered pre-orders for more than 3,000 bulbs since its debut on January 7th 2013. Their design consists of a circuit board with LEDs attached to it, folded up into the shape of a light bulb that plugs into a regular lighting fixture.

Thin Red Line Aerospace's products occupy the two extremes; space vehicles orbiting the Earth and balloons tethered to the bottom of the ocean. The Chilliwack, British Columbia-based company's website states that its staff has "experience spanning the decades following the Apollo program." Thin Red Line specializes in super high-tech products such as inflatable lunar shelters and inflatable shielding to protect spacecraft from radiation and micrometeoroids. An underwater balloon must be something these people design on a beer mat after a few pints. On their beer mat, the TRLA engineers scribbled a design for storing wind energy without expensive, bulky batteries by tethering huge balloons to the ocean floor near offshore wind farms. The wind turbines fill the so-called Energy Bags with compressed air that is released through electrical generator turbines when needed. The bags are tethered 600 metres below the water's surface where pressures are around 70 times greater than surface pressure. One Energy Bag can store about 14 hours of energy generation from the largest offshore wind turbine models. Balloons aren't the only inflatable product gathering energy from the sea. A UK company called Checkmate Seaenergy has designed a 200-ton, 650-foot long water-filled rubber snake called the Anaconda Wave-Energy Converter that uses the ocean's waves to generate power. As waves rise and fall, the Anaconda transfers this energy to a turbine generator that cranks out power.

Two Canadian companies have perfected technology to remove good stuff from toxic goo. Vancouver's Ostra removes phosphates and ammonia from waste and makes the high-quality fertilizer one might expect from poop. Titanium Corp of Calgary specializes in removing high-value minerals, like bitumen and solvents, at oil sands sites, keeping them out of the infamous tailings ponds, which now are the size of large cities. This makes the water easier to recycle and reduces the volume of water taken from nearby rivers and lakes. The bitumen and minerals are then resold into the market.

Malibu's Chris Goldbatt calls the ocean "my church." Goldblatt has occupied a number of positions in his church: deck hand, captain and sustainable seafood promoter. For the past 10 years, he has been a reef builder along the Southern California coast. Founder of the Fish Reef Project, Goldblatt skillfully drops what look like perforated concrete igloos onto the sea floor in polluted or overfished areas, which encourages marine life to re-settle on them. Over 500,000 reef balls have been deployed in 70 countries.

Hundreds of decommissioned oil platforms in the Gulf of Mexico are being used as marine sanctuaries for a wide variety of sea life. Studies have shown that marine life has exploded in the area since the oilrigs went operational. There are theories that pumping oil brings oxygen to deeper layers of the sea, and also warms up the water, allowing for coral and fish populations to grow. The retired rigs are also ideal to produce renewable ocean energy from wind, currents, waves and geo-thermal.

Calgary-based Carbon Engineering [CE] is a 2009 startup founded by Harvard Professor David Keith, the rock star of the cutting-edge physics world. He took first in Canada's national physics prize exam, won MIT's prize for excellence in experimental physics and was one of TIME magazine's Heroes of the Environment in 2009. CE is one of Bill Gates' pet greentech startups. The apparatus is simple enough: a narrow three-metre aluminum box open on both ends called a combine that works like a giant vacuum. Air is sucked into one end and flows the length of the box through corrugated plastic sheets. Carbon-trapping goo drips from the roof. The goo is sodium hydroxide that the carbon dioxide molecules stick to like dust sticking to the sweat on your face and the carbon soup drips onto the floor as carbonate salt. Everything gets recycled. The carbon dioxide is extracted as a pure pipeline-quality product — much like maple syrup is made from sap — and the now carbon dioxide-free goo is mixed with water to re-form fresh goo which goes back into the combine to capture more carbon dioxide. The sheer magic of the goo machine is the fact that the recycled carbon dioxide can be combined with hydrogen to create gas, jet fuel, or diesel. It is sweet irony that the oil industry will probably be one of CE's best customers. Oil companies often inject carbon dioxide into oil fields to force out extra oil.

URINICITY

Your pee is powerful. Scientists in England have built a machine that converts urine, the ultimate in sustainable raw materials, to electricity. They started small, with a cell phone, but talked, texted and web-surfed powered by half a litre of urine. Dr. Ioannis Ieropoulos led a team that figured out how to turn urine directly into energy using microbial fuel cells (MFCs), which contain live organisms just like those found in soil and the human digestion system. The MFCs digest the pee and produce electricity. Bill Gates is funding the next phase to see if the technology is scalable. This is a really huge step in the direction of a truly carbon neutral future where nothing goes to waste. Not even waste.

ITO'S OILFIELDS

In the early 1990s, I [Trevor] freelanced for a Tokyo magazine that was edited by Peter Fuchs, a passionate, fiercely intelligent American journalist with a relentless desire to go the extra mile for a story. He once went down to Kyoto and waited for three hours outside the home of the reclusive president of Nintendo to get an exclusive 90-minute interview. Occasionally, Pierre [as I call him] and I would meet after hours at a smoky workingman's pub under the railway tracks in central Tokyo. We'd drink beer, smoke cigarettes and solve all the issues of the day as the trains clattered by overhead. When I learned of a Japanese invention that converts plastic to oil, I immediately got Pierre to do some digging. This is what he came up with:

"We do it for the kids," says Akinori Ito, founder and president of a little company called Blest that is tucked away in the corner of an industrial park 40 miles west of bustling downtown Tokyo. Ito is now 54 and has three kids. "Without the help of the kids, we cannot turn this dream into reality," he says, "and it is to prove to the kids that they can do it that we developed our desktop prototype machines." [There are machines that convert plastic to oil but they are massive. Ito invented a home version that fits on a tabletop.] The dream is one he had as a much younger man, some 12 years ago when he looked around and saw oilfields all around the landscape in his native Japan. Not the kind you might find in Saudi Arabia or the Texas panhandle. Ito's oilfields are imaginary ones, as Japan has almost zero self-sufficiency in oil and natural gas. Ito's oilfields are in the vast mountains of processed plastic waste that Japanese households, fast-food joints and supermarkets churn out by the megaton. "The home is the oil field of the future," he says.

AN UNNERVING ABILITY TO STICK AROUND

Until the mass production of plastics began in the 1950s and 1960s, Ito explains, just about all the waste that mankind produced was readily recycled back into nature. But plastic is made from petroleum, from the same fossil fuels that are used to drive the modern industrial economy. [About seven per cent of the oil produced in a year is used for plastic manufacturing. This is higher than the oil consumption of Africa.]

Plastic is made in vast amounts that provide us with its benefits but also leave us with its curse. Modern plastics are cheap enough to throw away after a single use. Think of the cups and utensils you use at any fast-food restaurant from Anchorage to Zagreb and nowadays in almost every community on the planet. But though collected and buried in landfills with all other kinds of commercial garbage, plastic has an unnerving ability to stick around, as it does not readily decompose. "Those are my oilfields," Ito says. "I travel to many island countries like Palau and Micronesia to meet potential customers, government leaders, and non-profits. But unlike most visitors, I don't go there for the swimming or the skin-diving. I go there to see the landfills, to see what's in them, and how much is plastic." All of Blest's customers start with one of the Blest desktop models, which typically can process about 20 or so kilos of plastic waste in a day, and pump out about 20 litres or so of what Ito calls "plastic oil." The desktop machine is the size of a small suitcase and has the look of a piece of laboratory equipment from a high school chemistry class. The oven where the raw plastic scrap goes to is heated to about 500 degrees Celsius. The hot gases are vented into a water tank for cooling. The plastic oil floats to the surface of the coolant water and can be easily separated.

AN AUSTRALIA-SIZED PLASTIC OCEAN OF MISERY

Blest has developed a much larger one-ton capacity unit. "There is plastic waste everywhere on our planet," Ito says, "and sadly, much of it eventually ends up in the ocean." He knows fully well of the hidden shame of modern civilization, the vast ocean of floating plastic refuse that covers an area the size of Texas ("no, not Texas, it is the size of Australia," Ito says with some urgency) in the region known as the North Pacific Gyre, a maritime black hole that plastic waste floats into but never leaves. "It is a plastic soup," Ito says. Blest has been working with an oceanographic non-profit organization called the Clean Oceans Project that is hoping to build a prototype floating oil-conversion platform to operate in this vast ocean of misery. Customers come from around the world, with a relentless flow of requests for information. "They come in from all over, and we have distributors in places like Holland, India, Greece, Spain, Philippines, and the United States." Ito is excited about the prospects for the Blest technology on remote islands in the Pacific and emerging countries like Benin in Africa. But it is not just for the dustier corners of the world, where neglect and wanton waste have blown much of the world's annual plastic production (which Ito estimates at 250 million tons per year). The Pentagon has quietly been in touch with Ito to get a better sense of when the Department of Defense can begin to purchase and operate the plastic-to-oil machinery on their own. The Pentagon is the biggest consumer of fuel in the world.

THE MOTTTAINAI IMPERATIVE

The Kenyan environmental activist, Wangari Maathai, who won the Nobel

Peace Prize in 2004 for promoting conservation, popularized the Japanese term *mottainai* in her global campaigns. On trips to Japan, she would often gently chide her hosts for abandoning this long-held grassroots notion of "waste not, want not" that had been part of Japanese culture for ages. *Mottainai* was a word on the lips of every Japanese grandmother or parent until only a generation ago. Children were admonished to eat the very last grain of cooked rice, to use every pencil and notebook to the last, and whenever possible, to reduce, reuse and recycle. Even now, one can see elderly people fastidiously, almost reverently, hunting down the last grain of rice in their bowl. Tsunenari Tokugawa is the 18th descendant of the powerful Tokugawa clan that ruled Japan for some 250 years until the arrival of Commodore Perry and the resulting civil war in the early 1850s. "My ancestors gave up on waging war and focused on winning the peace," he said in a lecture in Tokyo. "The capital city of Edo [the ancient name for Tokyo] was a remarkable place under the benevolent rule of the Tokugawas and its great open-air markets also made it one of the cleanest most environmentally balanced cities in the world," he says. "Everything was bought and sold at the markets, and this is how Edo managed its waste. Just about every scrap had value to someone, and the notion of *mottainai* was on everyone's mind as a result." Waste has a darker and more sombre meaning in today's post-industrial world.

CORE TO THE FLOOR

There is a new and terrifying wasteland in the exclusion zone hastily evacuated after three of four nuclear fuel cores at the Fukushima Daiichi went into meltdown, a process eerily referred to as "core to the floor." Next to these still-smoldering nuclear reactors is a fourth, which was idle at the time of the March 11, 2011 tsunami. This one has a large cooling tank on its fourth floor that is full of spent fuel rod assemblies; potentially far more dangerous than their casual open-air storage facility would suggest. A loss of cooling water would trigger a runaway fire that would spew vast amounts of highly radioactive byproducts into the atmosphere. In 2013, two years after the massive earthquake and subsequent tsunami that wreaked havoc on the coolant systems at the facility, it looks like a war zone in some post-apocalyptic science fiction thriller. Thousands of workers toil to clear the site of its post-tsunami debris, to shore up its shattered infrastructure and pave the way for the decommissioning of the three damaged reactors on the site. Each worker is given a hazardous material-handling protective suit made of a fibre known as Tyvek, a material used for limited-use protection. Tyvek provides a convenient shield against dust and other air- or water-borne toxics, but is good for one day only. In the two years since clean-up operations on the Fukushima site began, a mountain of used Tyvek haz-mat suits has been quietly growing in a corner of the site. "Tyvek, you know, is made from polyethylene," Ito says, holding up a used Tyvek suit. "We have been working with one of TEPCO's [Tokyo Electric Power—the facility operator] subsidiaries and have successfully shown that our machines can safely process Tyvek and turn it into fuel that can then be used on-site to power various machinery," he says. Sadly, Ito and his team have no solution for the pressing problem of turning spent uranium fuel rods into something more useful or less hazardous, but they have found a clever method for once again helping people understand the real meaning of *mottainai*.

WAR AS A LABORATORY

For thousands of years, war has inspired inventions that become indispensible in peacetime. The Appian Way is a 2,000-year old masterpiece of Roman road building built to efficiently move troops that is still used today. German soldiers invaded Poland in 1938 driving Kubelwagens, the predecessor of the Volkswagen. The ubiquitous personal computer was designed as a code-breaking machine in the Second World War. The Internet was also conceived during the Cold War.

Medical advances were inevitable. After the US invaded Iraq, streams of money flowed to medical research facilities to study artificial arms and legs for amputees, creating the next generation of prosthetics. Dr. Hugh Herr of the Massachusetts Institute of Technology created a powered ankle and knee prosthetic with the gush of funds. "If you plot prosthetic limb technology you see a major spike in innovation after every war – except Vietnam – and this current conflict [Afghanistan] is similar in that regard," Herr said.

THE BIGGEST BOGEYMAN IN THE PACIFIC

As the top threat assessment officer in the Pacific, US Admiral Samuel Locklear keeps a weather eye on the many flashpoints in the region, such as the frenetic nuclear sabre-rattling of North Korea and the recurring tussle between China and Japan over an island chain both claim as their own, not to mention Chinese computer hacking; all excellent reasons to keep a couple of carrier battle groups at high readiness. But Locklear told the Boston Globe in March 2013 that in his opinion the biggest long-term security threat in the Pacific region is climate change. The Admiral's concern is borne out by the Arab Spring uprisings, which were only superficially political. The main driver was climate change–related crises. Food riots across the Middle East and North Africa in 2008 were sparked by a global rice shortage and steeper staple food prices. A month before the fall uprisings, food prices in Egypt and Tunisia reached record highs.

Trevor Greene and Mike Velemirovich

CHINA'S GLOBAL POWER PLAN

A FAR CRY FROM THE GREAT LEAP FORWARD

I [Trevor] remember being incredulous when I heard Beijing had been awarded the 2008 Summer Olympics. I was thinking of the athletes, the rowers especially, who would have to compete in a city that reeked of toxic fumes and whose inhabitants regularly had to wear surgical masks. While rowing at full speed, I had needed to gulp great lungfuls of fresh air and wondered how these world-class athletes would cope with the filthy, oxygen-deprived air. Beijing improbably managed to clear the air, so to speak, and air quality wasn't an issue. Typically draconian measures were put in place months before the games, including strict restrictions on vehicle use in the capitol, closing factories, halting construction projects, spraying roads with water to cut down on dust and regularly seeding clouds to produce rainfall. Although the controls were relaxed after the closing ceremonies, they significantly cut down the air pollution. A friend from my Japan days was transferred to the city in the mid-1990s, which is known to ex-pats as "Grayjing." He was reluctant to go, but it was considered a hardship post and the extra benefits eventually won Nathan over.

China has had an ignoble history of air pollution for over 50 years since Chairman Mao's Great Leap Forward from 1958 to 1962. Intended to free China from the need to import steel and machinery and catch up to the Western world, the brutal regime imposed on the Chinese people was in the words of one Hong Kong historian, "one of the worst catastrophes the world has ever known." At least 45 million people were worked, starved or beaten to death over those four years. By comparison, the death toll from the six years of World War II was 55 million. Mao forced peasants with no training in metallurgy to set up homemade forges, where they were to turn scrap metal and household items like pots and pans into usable steel. All they produced were huge mounds of low-quality pig iron and megatons of carbon dioxide. Over just a few years, the Great Leap Forward caused massive environmental damage in China. Thousands of hectares of forests were burned to fuel the smelters, which left the land open to erosion.

A modern-day "aircopalyse" choked Beijing in mid-January 2013. The highest quantities of smog the city has seen, since records began to be kept around 2008, blocked out the sun and filled hospital respiratory wards with gray-faced, hacking citizens. It was so bad, a fire in a furniture factory in Zheijiang province raged out of control for three hours before anyone even noticed. The International Herald Tribune said on January 13, the Air Quality Index at the US Embassy reached 755. Levels above 300 are deemed "Hazardous" and above 500 is "Beyond Index." On that day, the readings were at least 500 for 16 straight hours. The toxic cloud prompted one reporter to note, "All of Beijing looked like an airport smokers' lounge."

REDEMPTION

The Northeast seaside city of Rizhao is attempting to redeem China's legacy of environmental desecration. Rizhao means "first to get sunshine" and much of its 260 days of sunshine are gathered by rows of solar panels adorning nearly every rooftop. Photovoltaic solar cells power the traffic signals and street and park lights downtown. Virtually all the city's residents use solar energy for their hot water. Rizhao is the first city in China and one

Trevor Greene and Mike Velemirovich

of four cities in the world to make the commitment to go carbon-neutral. In 2007, Rizhao received a World Clean Energy Award for its green energy policy. Rizhao is the template city for China's great leap forward in renewable energy and the rest of the world is watching.

THE GREENTECH CRUCIBLE

Vancouver-based Westport Innovations has brought its signature technology to China; a high-performance, heavy-duty truck engine that runs on natural gas instead of diesel. In 2008, Westport formed a joint venture with Weichai Power, a heavy diesel engine-maker. The first Weichai Westport engine underwent road testing in 2012. China's market for environmental protection and energy savings technology is predicted to be worth $473 billion by 2015. "By virtually every metric that matters, China is the place to be doing business in cleantech these days," said Dallas Kachan, managing partner of a cleantech consultancy.

LanzaTech is a Chicago-based biofuel company. The firm's crown jewel is a super-microbe that converts carbon monoxide to fuel. LanzaTech has partnered with two Chinese steel manufacturers, Baosteel and Capital Steel, to turn waste gas from their operations into ethanol. Massachusetts-based GreatPoint Energy, a company that converts coal into cleaner-burning natural gas, signed a $1.25 billion partnership with industrial parts supplier China Wanxiang Holdings. The venture will build a plant that will take coal mined from the Gobi Desert and convert it to gas. By 2015, the plant is projected to provide around 0.5 per cent of China's energy needs.

BATTERIES AND BUILDING YOUR DREAMS

The technology to store electricity has been around for millennia. In 1938, small clay pots were found near Baghdad that contained an iron rod surrounded by copper plating designed to be immersed in electrical conducting fluid called electrolyte. These Baghdad Batteries are an astonishing 2,000 years old.

Allesandro Volta invented the modern battery in 1800 by stacking small plates of copper and zinc immersed in an electrolyte solution of heavily salted water. Battery technologies improved over time with the introduction of new metals and new electrolyte solutions, but challenges around limited energy capacities and dangerous chemical compounds remained. American physicist, Dr. John Goodenough, developed the lithium ion rechargeable battery in 1996 using an iron phosphate electrolyte solution. Iron phosphate is a compound of such low toxicity that it can replace pesticides in organic farming, which makes end-of-life battery disposal far easier. Iron phosphate batteries store about 15 per cent less energy than popular cobalt batteries, which means they must be a little larger. Their size makes them unsuitable for use in mobile phones, but it makes them ideal for cars and buses. They are cheaper than cobalt, but their primary advantage is life span. Where cobalt batteries can only be recharged only about a thousand times, iron phosphate batteries last for 6,000 cycles. This six-fold life span advantage means that after over a half million kilometres of driving in a car or bus, the batteries will still have thousands of cycles left.

EASTERN AND WESTERN BILLIONAIRES MEET
During the recession of 2008, legendary investor Warren Buffett invested $250 million in BYD, a Chinese manufacturer of iron phosphate batteries. A 29-year old chemist named Wang Chuanfu founded BYD in 1995. Wang's rice farmer parents died when he was young but he managed to earn degrees in chemistry and metallurgy. With a loan of $300,000 from his cousin, he founded BYD, an acronym for Build Your Dreams, and started manufactur-

ing rechargeable batteries for mobile phones. Within 10 years, he had captured a staggering 50 per cent of the global battery market. BYD launched its first plug-in electric hybrid car in 2008. Wang had a net worth of $5.8 billion in 2009 and was named by Forbes magazine as the wealthiest person in China. Most electric vehicle makers enter the car market with extremely expensive luxury sports cars intended for ultra-wealthy clients. Despite Hollywood glitz and racecar imagery, objections to electric cars remain, namely high cost and range anxiety. BYD attempted to calm these consumer worries by introducing relatively inexpensive electric cars for broad exposure to the public as taxis, rentals and police cars. BYD electric buses are used throughout Asia, Europe, and South America and have been introduced to North American roads in Ottawa and Los Angeles. In the spring of 2012, BYD successfully demonstrated a 40-foot battery pack at the Santa Rita high security prison in California. High security prisons, like hospitals, cannot be without power for even a minute, so they both need backup systems to kick in. The BYD power pack is charged by wind and solar energy whenever possible and by the conventional California grid using low-cost power at night.

A 60-YEAR HEAD START

BYD operates in China under a national energy plan that is updated every five years. By contrast, Canada and the US have been utterly unable to even set a framework for a national energy policy. As a result, market conditions tend to be influenced by special interests like Big Oil that rarely jibe with national interests. China is currently operating under its twelfth five-year energy plan, so they have a 60-year head start on planning the future of their energy sources. In order for western entrepreneurs like BYD's Wang to capitalize on the emerging renewable energy economy, governments must create policies that allow for the transition away from fossil fuel. These policies need to include clear objectives and logical energy subsidies. Fossil fuel executives in Canada and the US would be wise to participate in this process for two reasons. First because their long history of providing fossil fuel energy makes them uniquely qualified to provide renewable energy, so they stand to make a lot of money in renewable energy. The second reason can be summed up by the business axiom, "if you fail to take care of your customers, someone else will." And in the renewable energy economy that *someone else* is fast becoming China. The race for space between the US and Russia in the late 1950s saw extraordinary research and development followed by applied engineering that put humans on the moon in about 10 years. As fossil fuels become harder to extract and therefore more expensive and as climate change threatens our wellbeing, the world needs a call to Herculean action on par with the race for space. Ironically, in the race for renewable energy, China is fully engaged. North America, on the other hand, seems to deny the race even exists let alone acknowledge the urgency and heavy toll of losing. Governments and energy companies must take action and formulate policies and investments that make us competitive in the race for renewable energy. It is the ethical thing to do and it is good business.

INTERESTING TIMES WITH CHINA

There is a famous Chinese curse that goes "may you live in interesting times." When the government signed away control of our energy assets to China at the Asia-Pacific Economic Co-operation Summit in Vladivostok in September 2012, it ushered in an interesting time indeed. The deed was done on the last day of the meetings. This star-crossed treaty is called the Canada-China Foreign Investment Promotion and Protection Agreement (FIPA). MP Elizabeth May sent an energetic email in November 2012 that put the treaty into context: "for the first time in Canadian history, the Canada-China Investment Treaty will allow investors (including Chinese state-owned enterprises such as CNOOC or Sinopec), to claim damages against the Canadian government *in secret*, for decisions taken at the municipal, provincial, territorial or federal level that result in a reduction of their *expectation of profits*. Even decisions of Canadian courts can give rise to damages." May's request to the House Speaker for an emergency debate on FIPA on October 1st 2012 was denied. FIPA gifts one of the Northern Gateway pipeline's strongest proponents, national oil giant Sinopec, with the right to sue the BC government or any sub-national organization if it moves to block the pipeline. The "super-large petroleum and petrochemical enterprise group," as its website describes Sinopec, could even demand that only Chinese workers and materials be deployed on the pipeline project. In its annual report, Sinopec dispels any and all confusion as to its status; "Sinopec is state-owned company solely invested by the State, functioning as a state-authorized investment organization in which the state holds the controlling share." There is no rule of law in China. The Chinese Communist Party reigns supreme and its decisions are beyond appeal. FIPA could have been ratified in late October 2012, but it was delayed as a storm of protest erupted across Canada. CBC's Rick Mercer, never one to pass up the chance for a mighty rant, asked rhetorically if it was a scene from a James Bond movie. "Since when do Canadian prime ministers sign secret agreements with the Chinese in Russia? Was Dr. No there? Was there a naked lady painted in gold?"

Gus Van Harten is a global authority on investment trade deals and international arbitration panels. On October 16th 2012, Van Harten wrote an open letter to Prime Minister Harper urging a comprehensive review of FIPA. Van Harten painted a glaring picture of humble servitude if FIPA is ratified:

"the legal consequences of the treaty will be irreversible by any Canadian court, legislature or other decision-maker for 31 years after the treaty is given effect," Van Harten wrote.

CANADA LOSES THE FACEOFF

Financial Post columnist Diane Francis used a hockey metaphor to describe the FIPA deal in a November 2012 column; "Ottawa capitulated to China on everything. The deal ... allows only a select few to play on Team Canada on a small patch of ice in China and to be fouled, without remedies or referees. By contrast, Team China can play anywhere on Canadian ice, can appeal referee calls it dislikes and negotiate compensation for damages while in the penalty box behind closed doors." Francis compared the government's negotiating skills to those of the British Prime Minister whose strategy of appeasement led to Hitler's Nazis running roughshod over Europe. "The Tories, backed by a naive Canadian Chamber of Commerce and a handful of big, conflicted business interests, have demonstrated the worst negotiating skills since Neville Chamberlain."

In early 2013, the Hupacasath First Nation on Vancouver Island filed an injunction against the federal government, arguing Ottawa breached its constitutional obligations to consult First Nations when negotiating the FIPA. On the 27th of August 2013, the challenge was dismissed. Chief Justice Paul Crampton wrote that the potential adverse effects of the treaty that the Hupacasath submitted are non-appreciable and speculative in nature.

The online independent newsmagazine the Tyee has been tenacious in its coverage of the FIPA controversy, often using Van Hartens' analysis. Albertans Bev and Cole McKay wrote to the government with concerns about the treaty. They received a response from Conservative MP Blake Richards. The Tyee showed the letter to Van Harten and, on November 5th 2012, published his response to the claims made by the government in Richards' letter. We have reprinted it by permission of the Tyee.

Government claim #1:

Our Conservative Government is committed to creating the right conditions for Canadian businesses to compete globally. Canada's Foreign Investment Promotion and Protection Agreement (FIPA) with China — the world's second largest economy — will provide stronger protection for Canadians investing in China, and facilitate the creation of jobs and economic growth here at home.

Van Harten:

Chinese investment may facilitate the creation of jobs and growth in Canada. On the other hand, if it removes value-added benefits from Canada's resource sector or other areas of the economy, then it may undermine jobs and growth.

Government claim #2:

Our Government's ambitious pro-trade plan is opening new doors for Canadian businesses in dynamic, high-growth markets like China, and our FIPA with China provides important benefits for Canadian investors.

Van Harten:

Unlike NAFTA, the FIPA is not a trade agreement and does not reduce tariffs for Canadian exports to the Chinese market. Its main role is to protect Chinese-owned assets from legislatures, governments, and courts in Canada.

Government claim #3:

For businesses looking to set up in China, China cannot treat a Canadian company less favourably than they would any other foreign company looking to do the same.

Van Harten:

This is misleading. The treaty does very little to protect Canadian investors from discriminatory treatment in China and, in fact, it locks in an uneven playing field. Because China has more discriminatory laws and practices than Canada, the treaty freezes an unlevel playing field in China and a relatively level one in Canada.

Government claim #4:

Fundamentally, this investment treaty will help protect the interests of Canadians.

Van Harten:

Perhaps the treaty will protect Canadian interests. But on each of the key issues of market access, investor protection, and leveling of the playing field, the treaty favours China.

Government claim #5:

Creating a secure, predictable environment for Canadian investors is why, since 2006, our Government has concluded or brought into force FIPAs with 14 countries, and are actively negotiating with 12 others. The Canada-China FIPA is very similar to the other FIPAs that Canada is a party to.

Van Harten:

The Canada-China treaty is vastly different from Canada's other FIPAs with countries all of which invest relatively little in Canada.

Government claim #6:

In 2008, our Government announced that treaties between Canada and other states or entities, and which are considered to be governed by public international law, would be tabled in the House of Commons. Accordingly, the Canada-China FIPA was tabled in the House of Commons on September 26, 2012. This reflects our government's commitment to transparency and accountability.

Trevor Greene and Mike Velemirovich

Van Harten:

The treaty's constraints on Canada will last for 31 years, with major implications for Canada's relationship with one of the largest economies in the world. *Rather than release assessments and analyses of the treaty, however, the government has limited Canadians to about five weeks' notice of the treaty text with little opportunity for scrutiny and debate.* (Incredulous italics ours)

Government claim #7:

With regards to investor-state dispute settlement, it is Canada's long-standing policy to permit public access to such proceedings. Canada's FIPA with China is no different. All decisions of the tribunal will be made public.

Van Harten:

The federal government still has not released a NAFTA award in an important case that Canada lost in May 2012 [to Mobil Oil.]

Government claim #8:

It is also important to note that under this treaty, both Canada and China have the right to regulate in the public interest. Chinese investors in Canada must obey the laws and regulations of Canada just as any Canadian investor must.

Van Harten:

This is misleading. Both countries maintain the right to regulate in the public interest only to the extent that the arbitrators agree with how that right was exercised. The arbitrators have regularly rejected interpretations of these treaties that were proposed by governments, including by Canada. Van Harten said, "There is a real possibility that, over the lifespan of the treaty, Canada will face billion dollar-plus awards." Any disputes go before an international three-person arbitration panel, whose rulings are not subject to review in Canadian or international court. The arbitrators themselves aren't even judges, but usually heavyweight corporate lawyers, members of boards or moonlighting academics. Juan Fernández-Armesto is a respected Spanish arbitrator and university professor who is amazed that " ... three private individuals are entrusted with the power to review, without any restriction or appeal procedure, all actions of the government, all decisions of the courts, and all laws and regulations emanating from Parliament." International Trade Critic, Wayne Easter, forced the Conservatives to hold a briefing on the agreement by department officials on November 9th 2012. The government took only one hour to brief on an agreement that could apply for 31 years.

PROMISE FOR PLANET A

Sustainable energy holds promise for a cleaner world and promise for economic prosperity. When more governments around the world realize that their economies will flourish in a sustainable energy future, the inevitable conversion to renewable energy will be triggered. The perils of fossil fuel become more obvious every day as we foul our air, poison our water and push tides ever higher. A century ago, fossil fuel was popular because it was plentiful and cheap and allowed nations to rebuild after war and modernize life for millions of people. Decades later the unthinkable happened — fossil fuel began to run out. Oil and gas is now difficult to find and even more difficult to extract. While the debate over natural gas fracking rages on, the fact remains we must drill down five miles below farmland for noxious fumes to power our machines. Peak oil has long since been passed as reserves diminish and we must either squeeze oily sand or drill down miles below the floor of the deepest oceans in fragile, untouched ecosystems like the Arctic for ever more expensive oil. Billions and billions of dollars in tax subsidies flow every year to the American Big Oil companies, who regularly post billions of dollars in profits. President Obama's attempt in March 2012 to slash $4 billion in subsidies every year to the big five oil companies; Exxon, Chevron, ConocoPhillips, BP, and Shell, was thumped in the Senate. Exxon made nearly $4.7 million **an hour** in 2012. If even a fraction of this largesse were to be diverted to greentech firms, then the assertion made by legendary CEO of General Electric, Jack Welch, that "green is the new black" would be proven.

A century after he patented the alternating current motor that powered the War of Currents, inventor Nikola Tesla eloquently captured our modern dilemma: "We have to evolve means of obtaining energy from stores which are forever inexhaustible, to perfect methods which do not imply consumption and waste of any material whatever. If we use fuel to get our power, we are living on our capital and exhausting it rapidly. This method is barbarous and wantonly wasteful and will have to be stopped in the interest of coming generations."

The past 10 years have been the warmest in the 160 years that records have been kept. The biggest, loudest canary of them all fell silent in May 2013 and the silence is deafening. The highly precise analyzers atop the Mauna Loa volcano have been sniffing carbon dioxide above Hawaii for over half a century. The reading reached the highest level in three million years in the 24 hour-period ended at 8 p.m. Eastern Daylight Time on Thursday, May 10th 2012: **400** parts per million. It is long past time for us to realize that we are merely stewards of the Earth we will bequeath our children and grandchildren. The people of the Maldives are committed to carbon neutrality by 2020 and every child is educated in sustainability practices. There is an urgency there that can only be engendered by watching your homeland slowly being eaten away. We must all be Maldivians. We must all feel the seawater rising inch by inch on our ankles. We must all stand as one and rage against the soulless energy corporations pillaging our natural treasures with impunity. We must all rant at the spineless politicos slavishly doing their bidding. We must all roar to the greedy bastards brutally raping the only Earth we have: **not on my watch.**